THE DECISION TO SCALE

25 TIPS FOR WOMEN-OWNED BUSINESSES LOOKING TO GROW

Business Development Decisions Series

By Nancy G. Allen

Edited by Diane Sears, DiVerse Media, www.di-verse-media.com

Design and layout by Jill Shargaa,
Shargaa Illustration & Design, www.shargaa.com

DEDICATION

This book is dedicated to women business owners. I admire your courage, your commitment and your tenacity. Your ability to make an economic impact and your willingness to give back are what make you great. I appreciate the roles you play every day and am humbled to have learned from so many of you.

66

Luck is what happens when preparation meets opportunity.

— Roman philosopher Seneca

99

FOREWORD

When men aren't sure how to do something in business, they look around and find the person who is best at whatever it is, invite that person out for lunch or coffee, and ask for help and advice. They often end up being mentored, championed and sometimes even funded by the expert whose advice they sought.

In my experience, women are not as likely to reach out that way. We women are unsure about looking, well, unsure. We worry that if we appear to not know what we're doing, someone might think we're not competent or not take us seriously. That needs to change.

When my friend and mentor Nancy G. Allen said she was writing a book to help women-owned companies scale for growth, I knew she was the perfect person to do this. So many people I know turn to Nancy anytime we get to a phase of growth we haven't encountered before and don't know how to handle it. I've been in business for 20 years and have started or joined several small businesses, and I am happy to say I still turn to Nancy anytime I have a question.

This book could have been called "Ask Nancy." It's a compilation of tips on topics a business typically encounters as it's transitioning past the start-up phase. This is the time when business owners are poised for growth and have to ask themselves tough questions about whether they're personally ready, whether they have the right tools and processes in place, and whether they have surrounded themselves with the right people and have given those people the authority to handle some of the load.

It can be a scary time and feel a bit like stepping out onto a ledge. But with help and support from Nancy and people like her, women business owners can set up a safety net and feel confident about the adventure they're about to undertake.

I plan to keep this book on my shelf to use as a resource anytime I need to brush up on how to create a new strategic plan or I need a checklist for getting the most out of a conference, and I suggest you do the same. Some of the chapters are eye-opening, with concepts that are new to me, and others are good reminders of things I might have heard before but need to hear again right now.

It might not be the same as sitting down for lunch or coffee with Nancy, but it's the next best thing.

Enjoy!

Diane Sears
Founder and President
DiVerse Media LLC

INTRODUCTION

I have worked with more than 2,000 women business owners during the course of my career of 30-plus years in this space. In that time, I've been inspired and awed at the ingenuity, the vision and the tenacity of women. I have watched ideas blossom into multimillion-dollar businesses, and I've seen successful businesses fail and pivot and come back bigger and stronger.

Through it all, I've noticed that the decision to scale is really where the rubber meets the road. It's a tough decision and one that most owners face at about their third year in business. That's when most business owners realize that to grow their existing client base, they need help in the form of additional employees. Going from solopreneur to employer is a big decision, and scaling to become even larger is just as tough. The good news is that enlarging your team can help you double or triple your revenue. Even better news is that once you make the decision to scale and start to delegate, it gets easier.

This book contains a collection of chapters based on blogs for a business toolbox I published weekly to help our members develop their businesses. We've included some success stories and quotes to inspire you and to support you in your decision to scale your business.

The chapters are not necessarily meant to be read in order. You might choose instead to skip around to topics that are the most important to you at this point in your company's life. My wish is that you will keep this on your bookshelf or in your computer and refer to it when you need encouragement or a refresher on a certain topic and want to approach it with confidence.

You are not alone. We have a whole community of women business owners who can help you and guide you.

I hope you enjoy this book and that it provides you with lots of food for thought.

Happy reading,
Nancy G. Allen

TABLE OF
CONTENTS

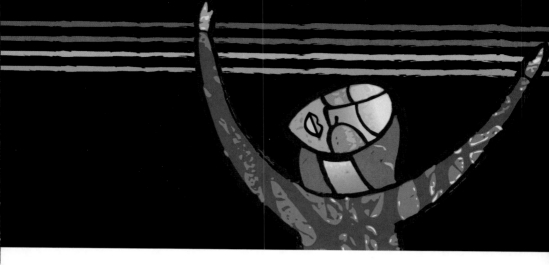

SECTION 1
PERSONAL
DEVELOPMENT

- THE INNER YOU
- OUTSIDE HELP

1

1

PERSONAL DEVELOPMENT

Before you consider all the options available to your business, including scaling to a larger enterprise, it's important to first examine why you want to do it. Who are you as an entrepreneur, and what do you want for your life?

There is nothing wrong with maintaining what's called a "lifestyle business," or one that supports you and maybe your family and even a few employees but stays the same size and is not focused on growth. Entrepreneurs all over the world find this satisfying.

But if you have a passion for growing your company, creating jobs, expanding your market share, increasing your revenues and establishing an enterprise that might become a legacy in your community or your industry, then scaling could be the right option for you. Scaling simply means taking what you do on a daily, weekly, monthly and annual basis and multiplying it all for growth that increases the size, revenue and reach of your organization.

In this first section, we examine some of the personal challenges you might be facing as a business owner and how to handle those. I've separated the tips into those that examine the inner you and those that look at how you bring in outside help for your personal development.
By following some of these tips, you can start your journey toward scaling from a position of strength, knowing you are personally ready.

▶ TIP #1

NURTURE YOUR SMALL BUSINESS PASSION

Did you start your business filled with passion? Did you see it as your life's calling, your purpose, what you were put here to do? If so, do you still feel that way? Do you still have a love of business ownership and excitement for it?

I serve as the CEO and president of the Women's Business Enterprise Council of Florida, a nonprofit that has been a champion of women-owned businesses since 1993. One of our missions is to connect women leaders and certify them through the Women's Business Enterprise National Council (WBENC). In my role, I get to work with women whose businesses are in all stages of development, from startup through mature growth through exit. I'll be sharing many of their stories throughout this book.

I still have a passion for my work after more than 30 years. That might seem like a long time for you, if your business is now three to five years old. What will keep you going for the next 25 years? What elements does your business need to have for you to feel that passion?

> ❝
> *Do what you love and success will follow. Passion is the fuel behind a successful career.*
>
> — Meg Whitman
> ❞

One of our members shared with me that she retired early from a successful career in computer information technology. She started looking at the carbon footprint she was leaving on Earth and how it was affecting future generations. In 2007, she founded a company that manufactures Earth-friendly products using rapidly renewable resources. Today she counts airlines, theme parks and retail grocery chains among her customers. Her business shows no signs of slowing down because she is passionate about her company's work.

"We believe in living responsibly and through our efforts making a positive impact on Earth," she told me. "We have successfully worked with major corporations, helping them to reach their sustainability goals by using our sustainable products. We are able to work through their complex supply chains to deliver the best sustainable products."

Research shows we will give it our all up to a certain point. That "point" looks and feels different for everyone. The chances are good that you know what that point is for you.

So, what can you do to keep up your energy about the business you own? A lot will depend on your specific circumstances, but here are eight ways to rekindle and nurture your passion:

1. **Define or redefine.** Ask yourself, "Am I doing what I set out to do?"

2. **Build your resilience muscle.** When was the last time you tried something new in your business? New market, new target goal, new client or prospect? When we try new things and explore new ideas, we force ourselves out of our comfort zone, and that builds resilience.

3. **Share your story.** Look critically at the "About Us" section of your website. Does it effectively communicate who you are and why you do what you do?

4. **Share your expertise.** Use industry keywords and language that is solution-based, not problem-centric.

5. **Know what you don't know.** Celebrate what you do know and get support for the rest. For instance, the time you spend learning how to design a perfect website when that is not your core business function is time you could be using to meet potential clients.

6. **Join a network for support.** Support can take on many forms — from coaching to consulting, from one-on-one sessions to group options to roundtables. You can join business groups like the Women's Business Enterprise Council of Florida (WBEC-FL), the Women's Business Enterprise National Council (WBENC), the National Association of Women Business Owners (NAWBO), Women Presidents' Organization (WPO), the Organization of Women in International Trade (OWIT) or many others. Business ownership can be lonely, whether you're a solopreneur or the head of a growing enterprise. Don't be afraid to seek support from your peers.

7. **Do something creative.** Paint. Take music or pottery lessons. Learn a new language. Do something that stimulates the right side of your brain. Stepping away from your day-to-day work can spark creativity,

and that will keep your passion alive.

8. **Keep your passion alive by keeping it top of mind.** You can easily do this by scheduling time in your calendar for reading and learning. The most successful business leaders read on a daily basis. Don't have time to read? How about listening to an audio book during your daily commute?

One of our members takes about four leadership training classes a year. The class duration ranges from one week to six months. When asked how she can manage to stay away from her business for that long, she asks how she can *not* afford to. She learns important information that she applies to her business immediately.

The classes also allow her to meet and network with other business owners, corporate representatives and top minds in her field and outside of her area of expertise. Another bonus she mentions is that she receives leads for business development. The result? An innovative and thriving business with engaged and loyal employees.

EXERCISE

In order to help clients really dive into their passion, I use the following exercise: Fill in the blanks for one of the following sentences, and do this at least three times, going deeper each time with your answers.

"I do _____ (what) for _____ (whom)
so that _____ (why)."

"I provide _____ (what) for _____ (who)
so that _____ (why)."

"I support _____ (what) for _____ (who)
so that _____ (why)."

❯TIP #2

UNDERSTAND WHAT MAKES A SUCCESSFUL PRESIDENT

For a long time, I've studied what makes a good leader in an entrepreneurial company. All of us are different, but effective presidents of small to midsize businesses that are scaling have some common traits. They also behave differently from their counterparts at companies that are not focused on growth.

Successful leaders aren't afraid to have the tough conversations that come with the job of president. They lead with empathy as well as strength. One of our members shared that the loss of a big contract forced her to make some tough decisions regarding staff members. Here's how she handled it:

She told the staff that the loss of the contract forced her to look critically at the business, and that led her to decide to move in another direction. She told the staff that the new direction would require new technology tools and expertise. Everyone had one month to come up to speed. Those who did would stay, and those who could not would have to move on. Her staffers appreciated that she gave them fair warning and the ability to learn and grow.

> *Stick to your true north — build greatness for the long term.*
> — Ruth Porat

Have you considered the following characteristics and behaviors and how they play into your role as the president and CEO of your company? The good news is that you are probably already doing at least some of these things. If you are doing all 10, congratulations! If you're falling short in some ways, there are resources available to help you.

1. Never stop learning. Successful small business presidents keep up with industry trends. They read articles, books and scholarly reports not only about their industry but also about other sectors. Keeping an open mind encourages creative and critical thinking that can lead to incredible breakthroughs.

2. **Brag about your success.** Your reputation is your legacy. Apply for awards, and when you get them, send out a press release. Include photos on your social media and your website. The simple fact is that people are impressed by your success, and your reputation is a good indicator of success. Ask for and offer to give testimonials. Be known – to your clients and your employees – as someone willing to learn from mistakes. Mistakes don't equal failure.

3. **Show support to your community.** Give back to your employees and your clients. Successful companies are those that show that they are committed to more than their bottom line. Are you passionate about a particular cause? Can you get your company behind that cause? Show your support by listing the charity on your website and letting everyone know that you will donate a percentage of your income to it. Consider allowing your employees paid time off to support their favorite cause. In addition to paying it forward, this will give you marketing and publicity that may attract new clients.

4. **Lead with integrity and authenticity.** Leaders know when something "feels" right or wrong. Have the courage to fire a client or a team member that does not fit well with your core values.
5. **Communicate regularly and openly.** How often do you have staff meetings? How often do you reach out to your clients? Your former

clients? Your potential clients? The most successful business owners report that they have regular staff meetings the same day, same time every week. This helps the team stay on top of goals and expectations. It also allows for time to course-correct when needed instead of when it might be too late. Reach out to your clients throughout the lifetime of the contract. Give brief updates and ask for feedback. Be intentional and tell your clients that they matter to you and you want to make sure you are delivering above their expectations. Very often, former clients will come back if you keep in touch with them. The key is to be seen and counted on as a resource. Make sure your communication is all about being of service rather than asking for business.

6. **Value your team members.** Successful presidents know their employees' strengths and how to fill the gaps on their teams.
7. **"Let go so you can grow."** This is a mantra I have invited small business leaders to incorporate in their day-to-day operations. In

---

RESOURCE

One of my favorite assessments is StrengthsFinder, which is now CliftonStrengths by Gallup. Use it to understand how to lead with your own strengths and how to celebrate the strengths of your team members.

---

other words, learn to delegate. You can't grow if you are working *in* your business instead of *on* your business.

8. **Show appreciation.** Do you know how the members of your team like to be appreciated? For some, a pat on the back will make a world of difference. For others, it's the constant feedback and time spent with you which will motivate them to go above and beyond.
9. **Clarify your vision.** Do you complete a strategic plan every year? Some small businesses have three-year and five-year plans. That's

great, but an annual plan allows you to course-correct and to be on top of goals because you can set up quarterly reviews.

10. **Lead through service.** Servant leaders incorporate all of the traits above and live in service to their clients, their team and their community.

How do you measure up? What would your team members say if I asked them whether you embody these traits? What would your clients say? You have an opportunity every day to make a difference through your leadership.

EXERCISE

Great leaders live by a set of values that guide their decisions and inform their choices. Core values can be personal and professional. Very often with small businesses, the personal and professional core values are interchangeable. These values or principles guide your company's internal conduct as well as its relationship with the world.

     Below are some common core values. Select three to five and start monitoring how they show up in your life. You will soon find that challenges you face are related to incongruity with your core values.

• Integrity	• Loyalty	• Positivity
• Ethics	• Commitment	• Optimism
• Respect	• Open-mindedness	• Passion
• Accountability	• Consistency	• Fitness
• Diligence	• Honesty	• Courage
• Perseverance	• Efficiency	• Education
• Discipline	• Creativity	• Patriotism
• Innovation	• Humor	• Service to others
• Drive	• Compassion	• Environmentalism
• Dependability	• Spirit of adventure	
• Reliability	• Motivation	

● TIP #3

BE AN INDUSTRY DISRUPTOR!

I once watched a pitch by the woman-owned business See Her Work that left me awestruck. It was at a Women's Business Enterprise National Council Summit and Salute conference, and as I watched, I realized I was witnessing an industry disruptor. Owner Jane Henry has designed personal protective work clothing and equipment to fit women, who traditionally have struggled in construction jobs and other positions that have required them to use men's work gear.

> "
> *I've never thought of myself as a female engineer, or founder, or a woman in tech. I just think of myself as someone who's passionate.* —
> Leah Busque
> "

Even if you don't become a disruptor, these seven common characteristics of disruptive leaders will help you to succeed in all areas of your business life:

- **Banish complacency.** Remember Blockbuster, Blackberry, Kodak and Sears Roebuck? Just because you are first to market doesn't mean you can rest on your laurels.

- **Be a lifelong researcher and learner.** Create focus groups within your own company to learn from people who are on the ground doing the job. One company I know gave each employee a budget of $1,000 and asked workers to share how they would spend it on improving efficiency and customer service. Don't have employees? How about creating a focus group made up of friends or colleagues? Most people will be very happy to help you out.

- **Show your clients how important they are.** Make a habit of asking for their opinions on your service delivery, designs and outcomes, as well as what isn't working for them.

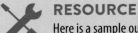

> **RESOURCE**
> Here is a sample outline or script for an outreach phone call:
>
> **You:** Hello, Jane. I hope you're doing well. I have a question for you.
>
> **Client:** Well, hello. It's good to hear from you. What's your question?
>
> **You:** I want to know how you like the latest designs we sent over. The team has been trying some new ideas, and I want to get your feedback. I really trust your judgment.

- **Reach out to potential clients.** Find people who don't buy your products and services and ask what would get them more interested. Don't forget to get a cross-cultural and cross-generational perspective.

> **RESOURCE**
> If you're looking for feedback on a product, service, procedure or something else, you might try setting up a focus group. This can be done in a variety of ways, from the formal method of bringing everyone into a room and having a facilitator ask questions to the more informal way of inviting a few key people to lunch. Focus groups give great insight and can save you time and money because they usually can spot some things you may not have considered.

- **Learn from outside your industry.** One of our members whose company is in the promotions space signed up for executive training with organizations focused on energy issues. She came out of it with a better understanding of how to run her business, a great group of business owners that she can target as clients, and knowledge on how to approach the energy industry with her products and services.

- **Ask for help.** See **Tip #6 Find a Mentor, Sponsor or Coach** for more information on how to find a mentor. If that's not possible, look for someone who is where you want to be and research how that person got there.

- **Be willing to take risks.** And be prepared to make the final decision. Be decisive, even if it means you might have to change down the road. Adopt a "Failure is an opportunity" mentality.

As Gillian Tans of Booking.com says: "Starting a business and building a product are not for the faint of heart. You have to learn to not let little disappointments get you down and to stay focused on the big picture."

NOTES

◗ TIP #4

USING MIND MAPPING TO GENERATE IDEAS

Mind mapping is like an enhanced version of brainstorming. Where brainstorming often lists ideas related to a concept, mind mapping invites you to show the connections between the different elements of the list. It's a visual representation of how our brains think in a non-linear fashion.

I'm a big fan of mind mapping in addition to brainstorming because I'm visual, and the process of drawing and connecting ideas and concepts appeals to me. It turns out that writing things down in a creative manner stimulates the synapses of our brains — and that means more creative *and* analytical thinking.

Some people combine brainstorming and mind mapping. The brainstorming part lists all ideas you have about a topic. You are generally encouraged not to overthink an idea when you write it down in a brainstorming session. You list everything you know about (fill in the blank). Mind mapping takes that one step further by inviting you to connect and create relationships between the items on the list.

> " I like to say it's an attitude of not just thinking outside the box, but not even seeing the box.
>
> — Safra A. Catz "

I came across a TEDx Talk by Hazel Wagner that gives an excellent overview of the concept and the scientific research behind the benefits of mind mapping. It's called "Want to Learn Better? Start Mind Mapping." She explains that remembering information and being able to retrieve it happens best when we're not just transcribing what we hear, but we are organizing the information in a way that is personal to us and helps us retain it.

MIND MAPPING

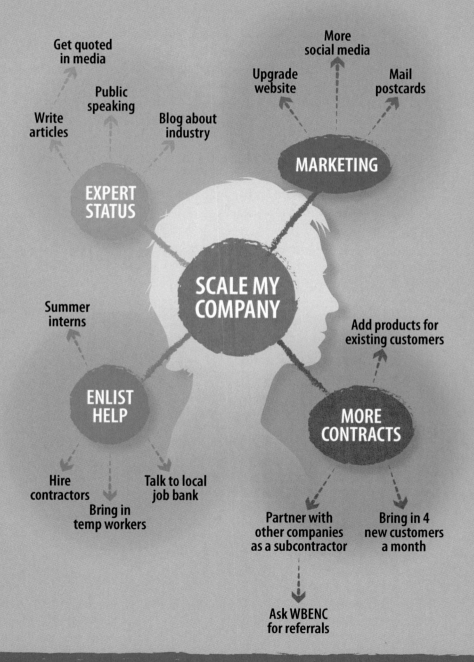

Get quoted
in media

Public
speaking

Write
articles

Blog about
industry

More
social media

Upgrade
website

Mail
postcards

MARKETING

**EXPERT
STATUS**

**SCALE MY
COMPANY**

Summer
interns

Add products for
existing customers

**ENLIST
HELP**

**MORE
CONTRACTS**

Hire
contractors

Talk to local
job bank

Bring in
temp workers

Partner with
other companies
as a subcontractor

Bring in 4
new customers
a month

Ask WBENC
for referrals

Here are some of the benefits of mind mapping:

1. Creative thinking is encouraged (and if you know me, you know I love creativity).
2. Everyone is invited to participate.
3. Drawing leads to open-ended questions and solutions.
4. It helps you look at a topic holistically.
5. It keeps the topic front and center — literally, because you put it in the center of the page and ideas radiate all around it.
6. It combines skills from both the left and right sides of the brain, using left-brain linear thinking and right-brain images and creativity.
7. It invites you to look at each item and ask how it relates to the others and the whole.
8. It allows you to visually identify the relationships between the ideas, such as by color, lines and shapes.

For those of you who want to do mind mapping electronically, you can find many apps and programs to download that will give you templates and formulas you can use. Whether you do it on paper or on a screen, you'll see how mind mapping can change the way you think and help you retain information long after you learn it.

◗ TIP #5

IDENTIFY YOUR ANCHORS AND ENGINES

We all know we should surround ourselves with people who lift us up. But why don't we do this? Sometimes it's difficult to tell whether a person is a positive in our lives or a negative because the truth is that most people can be both.

Let's look at some of the idioms that describe why it's important to surround yourself with people who will support you:

"You are the reflection of the five people you spend the most time with."

"A true friend is someone who reminds you of who you are when you forget."

> *One of the best things you can do is stop and listen; that's why it's good to not just immediately respond when someone talks to you. Just stop and make sure you internalized what they said.*
>
> — Lori Richardson

I've found these ring true for me on many different levels, and I'll bet you have, too. What can you do to determine whether someone is having a positive influence in your life?

I like to use the Anchors and Engines exercise first taught to me by my business coach Michelle Villalobos. It's meant to get you to look at the role the people closest to you play in your life. It's quite simple and very compelling.

Start by thinking about the word "anchor." What does that word bring up for you? Something that weighs you down? Something that keeps you in place? Something that provides you with safety? How about the word "engine"? What does that evoke? Moving forward? Speed? Progress? Creativity?

How do we define anchors and engines? Let's look at them this way:

Anchors: Negative things that are holding you back.

Engines: Positive things that are propelling you forward.

One of our members told me about a difficult conversation she had with her mother during the early stages of building her business. The two were the best of friends, but she felt her mother was often so critical about the way she approached her life and her work that the negativity was holding her back from honestly sharing her feelings with her mother. Her mother had become an anchor.

The member finally told her, "Mom, I'm serious about building my business, and I need to surround myself right now with positive people who will encourage me to move forward. If you can't be one of those people, I'm not going to be able to spend as much time with you."

The honesty worked, and her mother found positive ways to express her opinions, holding her tongue at other times when she worried her daughter was working too hard or not handling things the way she thought they should be handled. But she also offered solid advice anytime her daughter asked for it.

Another member told me about a different kind of difficult situation she faced when she became a mother just as she was just starting to grow her business. For many years, she had worked in high-profile corporate and nonprofit jobs, where parents had benefits that allowed them to take off with pay to spend time in their new roles. That is not always possible with entrepreneurship. This member said she struggled until she sought out people who could provide the empathy she needed. She was looking for engines.

"I have been very strategic in joining organizations and finding individuals who understand where I am as a business owner, a working woman and a mom," she told me. "That is what really helps on my toughest days, to be able to speak and be candid. I also have a practice to greet every day with positive thoughts and to say a moment of thanks every night."

EXERCISE

You're going to need a blank sheet of paper. Put a line down the middle of the sheet. On the left, write the word anchors. On the right, the word engines.

Now make a list of the 10 people you interact with most often. With the definitions we've established for anchors and engines in mind, place the names in the appropriate columns. Who do you turn to if you want help with a new idea or challenge? How does that person respond?

Let's say this person typically says, "Caution, caution! What if this? What if that?" That person probably falls into the anchor category. Then think about someone who responds with, "What a great idea! It's about time! What are you going to do first?" This person probably falls into the engine category.

This exercise is not an exact science. Some people will fall into both categories. And just because people are in one group or another, that doesn't mean they can't give you good and useful advice. I have plenty of anchors who keep me grounded and safe. I also have engines I call on to provide me with a push when I need it. My engines are my champions. They are the ones who "remind me who I am when I forget."

Go ahead. Make your list and observe your interactions. Were you right? Did you put the person in the correct category? How did that feel? How do you think your next communication will go?

Every time I do this exercise with a group, there are "aha" and awareness moments people share. For some people, the realization that they don't have either anchors or engines brings clarity and a determination that they need to work to change that.

What if you can't identify engines in your circle? Consider going to meetings of women's groups and organizations like Toastmasters. Consider joining a mastermind group where you can set goals and be held accountable for them on a weekly or monthly basis. Once you're aware of what you're seeking, you'll start to recognize engines and anchors in your life.

ANCHORS	ENGINES
_____	_____
_____	_____
_____	_____
_____	_____
_____	_____
_____	_____
_____	_____
_____	_____
_____	_____
_____	_____
_____	_____
_____	_____
_____	_____
_____	_____
_____	_____
_____	_____
_____	_____
_____	_____
_____	_____

▶ TIP #6

FIND A MENTOR, SPONSOR OR COACH

Have you ever wondered what the words mentor, sponsor and coach mean? Are they different? Yes. Is one better than the other? That depends on your goals. Are you looking for support, promotion or insight?

One of our members won a business pitch competition with a nice $20,000 prize. When she talks about the experience, she explains how important it was for her to rely on outside help to guide her through the growth of her business. This kind of help does not always cost money, and it doesn't always take a lot of time. It depends on the results you're seeking.

> *I've always been a bit of an introvert, but just because you don't fit the classic mold doesn't mean you can't be a leader. You just need to find your own style and someone with a similar style who you can learn from.* — Jess Lee

This member tells her story this way: "I was matched up with someone from the company that sponsored the event who helped me make changes and innovations to my business, which was a nice bonus. But the best thing that happened was that I got to meet his network. That took my business from less than $1 million to over $2 million in the year I worked with him. I followed everything he told me, and most importantly I learned the power of working with a network of people who can expose you to others beyond your own group. Some of the ideas I implemented came from people in industries not at all related to my own."

This person acted as both mentor and sponsor. How do you identify the different types of relationships that can help you scale your business, and where do you find people to fill these roles? Let's explore each kind of relationship so you can determine which one might be best for you at this point in your personal development. It's possible you might need all three during some points in your career.

THE MENTOR RELATIONSHIP

I have had mentors over the years, and I've been a mentor. In all honesty, some of the relationships worked and others did not. There are books, courses, articles and firsthand accounts on how to find a mentor and how to mentor well. There are some key elements from the perspective of the mentor and the mentee that must be considered and put in place for the relationship to flourish on both sides. Here are some ideas for you to consider.

Five questions to ask yourself before you enter into a relationship with a mentor:
1. Why do I want a mentor?
2. Am I open to accountability?
3. Will I take advice and criticism well?
4. Can I commit to this? For six months to a year or more?
5. Will I be able to end this relationship if it is not working out?

Four questions to ask a potential mentor:
1. Have you mentored someone? How was the experience?
2. How much time can you devote to mentoring me? Six months to a year? How often can we meet?
3. Can you help me with...? (Fill in the blank with your need. The more specific you are, the more likely you will get a positive response. If people say they can't help you because they don't have experience or contacts for what you're looking for, consider asking them if they can recommend someone.)
4. What would you expect from me as your mentee?

It is essential to keep in mind that mentorship works best when there are benefits for both parties. What are you bringing to the table? How can you make this enjoyable for the person mentoring you? Be prepared to present those answers when you first meet with a potential mentor. Be intentional. State your dedication to your advancement, and promise to devote time and effort to get there with that person's guidance. Don't be afraid to say that you admire that person and want to be like him or her, hence the request.

You should also be prepared to hear, "I'm sorry, but I can't help you at this time." As hard as that is to hear, appreciate the other person's honesty, and consider it a positive thing. It means that the relationship would probably not have worked.

Here are some ideas on where you can find a mentor:

- **Within your former company**. Before you started your business, you likely developed relationships where you worked before.
- **Within industry groups.** Is there someone you admire in your industry who would not be considered a competitor?
- **Online.** Many organizations and businesses can help you find a mentor. The listings are by category, by experience or by location, for instance. Some of these offerings are free and some charge a fee.

Asking for help opens the doors to so many possibilities. A good mentor will hold you accountable and will offer new ideas and new ways of thinking of things. Key to your success will be the objective evaluations a mentor will present. Equally important is the creation of a safe space where you will have the opportunity to let your guard down. And that is what opens the door to your creativity and ultimately to your success.

THE SPONSOR RELATIONSHIP

A sponsor is a person of power and influence who champions you and intentionally promotes you to decision-makers within an organization. Keywords associated with sponsors are "advocate," "power to make a difference," "supporter" and "promoter." Also important to remember is that the sponsor/sponsored relationship is *different* from the mentor/ mentee relationship because it is transactional. Both parties must give and get.

> "
> *Mentors give you perspective while sponsors give you opportunities*
>
> — Cate Huston
> "

One of the best resources (in my opinion) that outlines the difference between mentors and sponsors is Sylvia Ann Hewlett's book *Forget a Mentor, Find a Sponsor: The New Way to Fast-Track Your Career.* Her writing is full of research, statistics and data that not only highlight the differences but make the case as to why you should have a sponsor and how to get one.

Key to the process is knowing that the professional sponsor/sponsored relationship is one of *mutual* benefit. Where *mentors* give you advice and knowledge and (generally) don't expect anything in return, career *sponsors* will go out on a considerable limb for you when they know your success will reflect well on them.

Here are some takeaways from Hewlett's research:

- **A professional sponsor relationship is transactional.** Women tend to look for sponsors who are just like them, and this is not necessarily the best fit. You don't have to like the person, but you should respect him or her.

- **The relationship must be genuinely reciprocal.** You need to earn sponsorship.

- **Build your case before you approach a potential sponsor.** It is imperative that you show and be intentional about how you will make your sponsor shine.

- **Consider the relationship like a strategic alliance.** Make the sponsor look good so that furthering your career advances that person's career or standing.

How and where can you find career sponsors? Here are some ideas:

- Network at places where you will rub elbows with influential people.

- Join nonprofit or philanthropic organizations where you can get to know people of influence who share your passion for a certain cause.
- Reach out to people you admire and be intentional about building

rapport. You know the adage "People do business with people they know, they like, and they trust." The same is true with sponsors.

• Consider converting a mentor into a sponsor. Mentorship allows the person to get to know you. Once you have taken that person's advice and advanced, you can approach a mentor and ask him or her to sponsor you. As outlined above, the sponsor role is more public and proactive. Don't forget to describe and demonstrate what you bring to the table that will make it worth that person's while to sponsor you.

66

A sponsor is someone who will use his or her internal political and social capital to move your career forward within an organization. Behind closed doors, he or she will argue your case.

— Jo Miller

99

THE COACH RELATIONSHIP

The first thing to know about coaching is that there are as many types of coaches as there are reasons to see them. We are long past the days of catch-all coaches and more into a time of niches and specialties. Did you know that there is a big market for sleep coaches? How about parenting coaches? Both are in high demand because productivity is top priority these days, and you can't be productive if you're sleepy or stressed out about your kids.

We are also (thankfully) long past the days of thinking that coaching was a perk for people at certain career levels. Anyone can work with a coach.

Here are 10 ways a good coach can help you:

1. New perspectives
2. An objective way of looking at a challenge
3. Setting goals
4. Accountability
5. Unbiased sounding board
6. Fostering and promoting creativity and creative thinking
7. Support and encouragement
8. Identifying strengths and weaknesses
9. Increasing self-confidence
10. Resources and referrals

I once heard that Oprah has five coaches. You might think that's a lot, but truth be told, it's the right number for her and (true confessions) for me, too. Yes, I have five coaches: a business development coach, a physical trainer, a spiritual coach, a leadership coach, and a TED Talk coach. I'm a firm believer in accountability, and I know there are people out there who can help me achieve my goals with a shorter learning curve.

Depending on the niche, you'll want to ask different questions of a prospective coach. For example, you would want to ask a business development coach about success rates in terms of revenue or client acquisition. A physical trainer/coach must be able to answer questions about equipment, diet and exercise, and techniques to be used to meet your weight loss or strengthening goals.

No matter what type of coaching you seek, you must have a connection or rapport with a coach. You must have a positive feeling about this person because without that, you will not get what you expect or paid this individual to do for you.

How do you know if you and the coach will click? If the prospective coach doesn't offer a strategy or discovery session, ask if you can schedule one. These are usually free of charge, 30 to 45 minutes long, and will give *you* insight into the coach's style, methodology and personality.

As a coach, I always offer a complimentary strategy session, where I get insight into the client's needs and expectations. My philosophy is that my clients know what they want and need, and my role is to be a guide and resource provider. When it comes to coaching, I'm definitely in the "show a man how to fish" camp.

Yes, you can probably do anything on your own if you really focus. However, working with a good coach will help you enjoy the process, learn new techniques and establish a safe space to try new things, assess success and step out of your comfort zone.

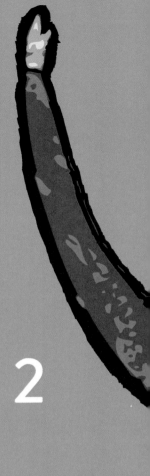

SECTION 2
BUSINESS DEVELOPMENT

• MASTER MARKETING
• KEY RELATIONSHIPS

29

BUSINESS DEVELOPMENT

U p to this point, the business has been your "baby." You've given birth to it and have nurtured all aspects of it to help it grow. Maybe you've already hired employees and are looking to bring on more, or you're considering hiring your first people. What will they help you do?

This section of the book addresses how you will bring in more clients. As you enlarge your pipeline of clients and contracts coming in, you'll want to expand your team to be able to handle fulfillment of the additional work.

The first part of this section deals with the marketing you'll need to put in place to increase the number of contracts you bring in by widening your company's influence and reach. It will take a lot of work to set up and maintain these marketing efforts, and that's one place where you'll be able to use the help of your employees and maybe even some contractors.

The second part of this section is about key relationships you'll want to continue developing and growing, including those with potential buyers at large enterprises such as corporations. If you establish these relationships effectively from the beginning, they will help your company through all of its future phases of growth and expansion.

IDENTIFY NEW BUSINESS TRENDS

Are you providing the same kind of service to your clients as you did two years ago? Are you making the same products as you were three years ago? There is value in stability and consistency, but when you don't evolve, you run the risk of stagnating and losing market share.

I have a client who tells the story of how she got into the business she runs. She was working for someone else when a customer came in and had a special request. Her boss said, "No, we can't do that." She followed the customer out and offered what seemed to be an unorthodox solution. The customer said, "Yes, because I'm desperate." The solution worked, and that led to referrals and a whole business that now employs 50 people and has revenues in excess of $5 million.

Her advice? When you are offered a gift, open the package. She credits her success to being in the right place at the right time and stepping up with open arms to embrace a challenge.

One of the keys to business success is to place yourself in a position of thought leadership. And one of the best ways to get there is by identifying trends and acting on them in a way that positions you as "the" best resource, manufacturer or solutions provider. How do you identify new business trends? It's a lot easier than you think.

> *I always did something I was a little not ready to do. I think that's how you grow. When there's that moment of 'Wow, I'm not really sure I can do this,' and you push through those moments, that's when you have a breakthrough."*
> — Marissa Mayer

Ten considerations if you want to stay top of mind to your customers:

1. **Accept and embrace change.** This is important. As a business leader, your attitude toward change will set the tone within your business. Strive to promote discussions with people who are key to your organization, such as staff members and vendors, about what they see on the horizon.

2. **Be curious and ask questions.** Put the topic of trends on the agenda of your next staff meeting. Have an open forum where you encourage questions about how the company does things and why. Could there be a different way? What is the competition doing? I was at a meeting with representatives from the major auto makers about five years ago. The topic of conversation was whether people would still be buying cars in 15 years. They discussed whether people will want to go into a dealership for regular car maintenance or instead expect the service to come to them. One of the attendees said those in the industry are moving from considering themselves as automakers to being in the logistics business.

3. **Get advisors.** Join a mastermind group. Surround yourself with other business owners who are willing to share ideas.

4. **Follow industry publications and influencers.** Read industry publications and follow the authors writing in them. When you go to conferences, write down the names of people speaking and connect with them online.

5. **Use tracking tools like Google Trends.** What are consumers or customers researching online? Keywords can reveal interests or problems or issues that need to be solved.

6. **Understand the difference between short-lived fads and long-term trends.** Decide where you want your company positioned. Remember the Pet Rock? Someone made a lot of money for a short period of time. But then what?

7. **Use focus groups.** Ask your existing clients what is working for them and what you can improve. A simple question like, "What can we do

to make this better, easier or more convenient?" can open the floodgates for ideas. Your clients will be flattered you asked their opinion. When my nephews were in high school, they participated in focus groups for companies that produced products targeting young adults. My nephews were happy to participate because it meant getting a firsthand look at some new products, and they were paid for their advice. Who does your business target? Can you reach out to a local college or university and ask whether students can participate in a focus group?

8. **Read!** Read everything: local newspapers, magazines, industry reports, even self-help books. Don't like to read? Listen to podcasts or watch TED Talks. The point is you have to stay informed.

9. **Block out creative thinking time.** Take a hint from some of the greatest minds who say an idea came to them when they were away from the office.

10. **Network where your clients' clients go.** Spot trends that your clients might not yet see and offer a solution they can use.

It's essential to also look at the big picture. Watch customer reactions through a local, national and global lens. Look at demographics. Pay attention to the role of technology — is there an additional role or application on the horizon? Consider social factors. Stay on top of current events. It's all interrelated and connected.

I've noticed some trends in auto dealerships and vehicle maintenance shops. They're incorporating more perks for customers in their waiting rooms. My local mechanic's shop offers free coffee and popcorn, a variety of great magazines, and a couple of different TVs as well as quiet rooms where you can take phone calls or work on your computer. There is a shuttle that will take you home and pick you back up when your car is ready. Someone told me her dealership has a movie theater with new releases playing for people who are waiting for their vehicles to get serviced. These examples show the industry is looking at what its customers want and finding a way to serve them better. Your company can find ways to do this, too.

◗ TIP #8

HAND OUT A MEMORABLE BUSINESS CARD

I'll admit I'm old-fashioned when it comes to professional and business norms. How old-fashioned? I still use business cards, and I always keep hard copies of the ones I've entered into our electronic database. Why? I like to see and touch and visually remember who I met and when. I'm the person you meet who reads and comments on your card.

"Nice colors," "Clever title" and "Great photo" are some of the things I'll say when I meet you. And if you seem receptive to suggestions, I might offer them to you right there on the spot. I'm not a graphic designer or a business marketing specialist, but I do have a good sense of what works visually. Let's face it, I've seen a lot of business cards in my time — enough to make me more of an authority than most people.

> *Your value will be not what you know; it will be what you share.*
>
> — Ginni Rometty

In my experience, the best cards have five key elements — in addition to the standard contact information, of course. Once you have these in place, you can add some more personality.

Five things great business cards have in common:

1. **Enough blank space that I can jot down some notes.** I may want to write down where we met and what I promised to send you. The best cards are uncoated ones that you can write on.

2. **Good and sturdy card stock.** No flimsy I-printed-it-on-my-computer cards, please. Your card has to go from your hands to mine and from my hands to my pocket or my purse. Sturdy stock means it won't look like a wrinkled shirt when I pull it out again. It will look clean and crisp, which is how you want me to remember you!

3. **A clever tagline.** This is especially important if the name of your business doesn't say what you do or who you're targeting. Help me remember the former and the latter, and you're more likely to get a call or referral from me.

4. **Easy-to-read font.** The older we get, ahem, the harder it is to read the small print. Combine small print with a cursive font, and chances are your card will not be in my keeper pile. It might even make it to the cards I use with my coaching clients under the heading "What not to do."

5. **A nice photo of you.** We all come home after networking events intending to immediately enter and categorize our new contacts, but this rarely happens. Days and weeks might go by before people start formal follow-ups. And guess what? Your card will probably look no different than the 20 other cards with no photo. Were you the one with the glasses? Or the one who had long hair in a French twist?

As an aside, if you are certified by the Women's Business Enterprise National Council (WBENC) or you hold any specialized certifications or industry-related affiliations that are important to mention, take advantage of the marketing edge you'll get by including those types of logos on your business card.

Take a look at your own business card. Does it portray your business in the best possible light? Does it leave people receiving it with the impression you want them to have? Does the person who receives your card know what you do? Is it time for a refresh or for a whole new look? The good news is that there are plenty of creative people out there who can help you.

I always get compliments on my business card. It shows me holding a sign that says "Make Allies and Believers." The big bonus is that it allows me to tell the story behind the sign. The story is memorable, and the saying is inspiring. What can you put on your card that will help tell your story and make you and your company memorable?

▶ TIP #9

CLAIM EXPERT STATUS

If you want to make a big impression on people who are potential clients and persuade them to think about hiring your company, they need to see you as an expert in your field. Think about what you look for when you hire someone. You don't want a person who's just starting out in the construction business to handle the remodel of your home. You don't want a brand-new mechanic fixing the brakes of your car without someone who's an expert supervising the job. Your customers are the same. They want an expert.

> " *At the end of the day, you are the only one that is limiting your ability to dream, or to actually execute on your dreams. Don't let yourself get in the way of that.* — Falon Fatemi "

How do you claim expert status? Even if you're fairly new at your business, you probably have more experience than you think. Take stock of how long you've been doing what you do. It's not only how many years you've owned the business that counts. Highlight your direct and related experience as well.

Nine ways you can establish expert status:

1. **Are you the first, only, original or most?** It's about branding. Think about it. Were you the first in your city? Are you one of the X% of women-owned businesses in your industry? Find out what sets you apart and use that to your advantage. Be consistent in your branding.

2. **Write a white paper.** A white paper provides information about a product or process. Does your company have a particular process or philosophy that you can teach others? A white paper does not have to be hundreds of pages long. An excellent PowerPoint presentation can work as a white paper. One of our members manufactures a specific product that is produced overseas and imported to the U.S. She wrote a white paper in the form of an animated PowerPoint presentation that detailed the manufacturing

process. This gave potential clients confidence that the product was being produced according to expected standards and also showed that her company was on the cutting edge of technology.

3. **Write a book.** Don't panic. It does not have to be a dissertation. A book can be a collection of interviews. It can be an e-book or a self-published hard copy book. You can do a "how to" book or write about the history of your industry. And P.S., there are a lot of great ghost writers and coaches out there who can help you if you don't feel confident writing it yourself.

4. **Become a speaker.** Public speaking is an excellent way to become known as an expert in your field. Nervous about public speaking? Join Toastmasters or other speaking development groups. The more you practice, the more comfortable you will become. I imagine that you know a lot about your business or industry. Why not share that knowledge? And you don't have to wait to be asked to be a speaker. Offer yourself to local groups that are looking for educational or informative programming for their members. I've gotten a lot of speaking opportunities by letting groups know I am local and available on short notice if their speaker backs out at the last minute. I always include a list of topics and at least five takeaways that audiences will get from the presentation.

5. **Become a guest columnist.** Local newspapers and magazines, and especially industry publications, are always looking for guest columnists. It means less work for them if they know they can count on you. Offer to interview local business owners about the economic climate, job opportunities, trends and new ideas.

6. **Sign up for HARO (Help a Reporter Out).** This is a great organization that allows you to register as either a reporter or a resource. Reporters will contact you for quotes, opinions, ideas and background

information. As a writer, you can contact other people for resources and information that can help you with white papers, books and published articles.

7. **Get involved with industry groups.** In addition to your industry, why not get engaged with ancillary industries? How about industry groups where you have business targets? For instance, if your business is in cabinetmaking, why not join a group of people in real estate so members can refer you and you can refer them?

8. **Get involved with community groups.** What are you doing in your community that is remarkable? Do you volunteer? Do you give your employees time off to volunteer? Highlight the toy drive you hold during the holidays. Highlight the interns you use from the local high a school or college. The more visible and active you are in your community, the more your neighbors will want to use your services and refer you.

9. **Become an adjunct professor at a local college.** Colleges and universities are always looking for adjunct professors. You gain as much as you give. You learn and grow by staying abreast of trends and new ideas. Showcase your talent at your local college, and you might even be able to identify your next star employee there — not to mention that there is something to be said about the title "professor."

Claiming expert status is much easier than you think. Get started today and continue developing your expert status as you grow your company.

❯ TIP #10

CREATE AN EXCELLENT CAPABILITIES STATEMENT

When you approach corporate buyers about doing business with your company, they might ask you for a capabilities statement. This is a document that provides background information about your business and what kinds of services or products your company offers. It should be in a one-page format and give a quick overview of your business so it can be read and understood easily and quickly. What goes into it?

> *You need to fully believe in yourself and your capabilities for others to believe in you.*
>
> — Anuranjita Kumar

The 12 elements of an excellent capabilities statement:

1. **Contact information.** Include your name and title, your address and phone number, your email address, and your website with a hyperlink.

2. **Business description.** Be brief, include the year you established your business, describe your products and services, and outline the unique qualities of you and your company.

3. **Photograph.** Make sure you have an up-to-date photo. This should be a professional headshot or an environmental portrait of you and your team or the company.

4. **Geographic reach.** Include locations where you provide services. Are you local, regional, national or global?

5. **Expertise.** Be sure to cover your areas of expertise by providing a list or writing it out in narrative form.

6. **Differentiators.** How are you different from the competition?

7. **Customers or clients.** Provide a list of your customers or clients, and be sure to give contact information. Your list should mirror your target audience.

8. **Awards and commendations.** Make sure to list your awards so you can assert your bragging rights. List relevant individual honors as well as company awards.

9. **Key personnel.** If you include key personnel, make sure the qualifications are a fit and be sure to add titles and areas of expertise.

10. **Industry codes.** It's essential to provide a list of your industry codes. Include your NAICS codes, listing those that are primary and secondary to your business.

11. **Certifications.** Be sure to include any minority certifications, gender-based certifications and industry certifications. Also include certifications with your local and state governments.

12. **Your branding and logo.** All of your corporate documents and marketing materials should have the same look and feel.

Remember to tweak your capabilities statement to fit your target audience. It is OK to have several versions that you use depending on who you're targeting. Not all information will be equally relevant to all of your potential customers.

And remember to research the company you're targeting and mirror the language you see in its marketing materials and on its website. This will help make your capabilities stand out more as a great fit.

CAPABILITIES STATEMENT EXAMPLES

FRONT

CAPABILITIES STATEMENT

WHO WE ARE

Corporate Fitness Works is a premier provider of fitness center design and management. Our fitness solutions are tailored to meet the unique needs of employees who work in today's large-scale office environment. Established in 1988, we have over 30 years expertise in engaging working populations in healthy, active lifestyles.

Companies of diverse size and industry partner with us because we know how to combat big health risk drivers that are common to corporate life; like sitting too much and stress. We have a national presence and are the largest certified, woman-owned provider in our field.

We are customer focused and have satisfaction ratings to prove it. Our management goes far beyond folding towels, and our programs are about much more than logging miles. We are your partner in driving a positive company culture and getting to the heart of what helps your organization attract and retain healthy, productive employees.

600+
EMPLOYEES

21
STATE LOCATIONS + D.C.

#1
AWARD WINNING IN
BUSINESS & INDUSTRY

98%
NATIONAL
SATISFACTION RATING

100+
CLIENT SITES MANAGED

70k+
DESIGN & MANAGE
SIZES FROM 1K - 70K SQ FT

WHAT WE DO

FITNESS CENTER MANAGEMENT
- Member recrtuiment, enrollment & retention
- Daily operations, policies, & procedures
- Professional fitness staffing
- Fitness consultations & assessments
- Personal training
- Group exercise classes
- Recreation programs
- Facility cleanliness & maintenance
- Education & outreach programs
- Safety & risk management
- Utilization & satisfaction reporting

FITNESS CENTER DESIGN
- Market demand & feasibility study
- Business plan & projections
- Facility design & layout
- CAD drawings
- Program operations & development
- Equipment recommendations & layout
- Full-service procurement
  (order, delivery, install)

We work with all major fitness suppliers and equipment brands.

BACK

OUR LEGACY AND LEADERSHIP

Our roots began in 1984 when two industry pioneers, Brenda Loube and Sheila Drohan, started to work with our first corporate client, Sprint. We've since cultivated our fitness center management expertise by working with corporate clients of all sizes and industries. These experiences have powered us to stay ahead of trends, technologies and creative ways to offer unique service to our clients.

Now owned by Beth and Michael Vivio, CFW manages more than 100 clients sites in 21 states, and remains as the largest women-owned business in the fitness management industry. Beth and Michael have extensive leadership experience with a laser focus on driving innovation and further expanding CFW's geographic footprint. As Chairman of the Board and President, Beth holds majority ownership and maintains CFW's certification status as a WBE and MBE through Women's Business Enterprise National Council (WBENC) and the National Minority Supplier Diversity Council (NMSDC).

*CFW Owners
Beth and Michael Vivio*

NAICS Codes	
713940	Fitness and Recreation Sports Centers (primary)
621999	All other miscellaneous ambulatory health care services
611430	Professional and Mgt. Development Training
541611	Administrative Mgt. and General Mgt. Consulting Services
611620	Sports and Recreation Instruction
721110	Hotels and Motels
812990	All other personal services
UNSPSC Codes	
91101501	Health and Fitness clubs
49200000	Fitness Equipment
49201606	Fitness Weights
85122200	Individual Health Screenings and assessment services
D&B Number	79-908-2334

For more details
visit website here

Contact Us
BusinessDevelopment@teamcfw.com | 866-417-9697 | CorporateFitnessWorks.com

f y in ⌾ p t

**Powerful Impressions
Are A Reflection Of Our
Commitment To Excellence.**

LANE HICKEY-WIGGINS
PRESIDENT/CEO

Lane Kathryn Hickey-Wiggins is the President and CEO at Dprint. Armed with a degree from SCAD (Savannah College of Art and Design) and an MBA from USF, she's passionate about advocating for women in business. She holds Board of Director positions for Go For The Greens and SGIA (Specialty Graphics Imaging Association). She is a member of the Women in Print Alliance as well as the Sustainability, Safety, Health, and Personnel Committee hosted by SGIA. She is also an active board member for the Junior Achievement Advisory Board of Polk County and for Explorations V Children's Museum.

MICHAEL HICKEY
VICE PRESIDENT & PRODUCTION MANAGER

Michael J. Hickey is Vice President and Production Manager of Dprint. Hickey began his career in 1981 at Atlanta Creative Graphics. He joined Douglass Screen Printers in 1984 as the Production Manager. Michael has two years advanced education from Auburn University and Polk State College. He is pursuing a degree in photography from the Art Institute of Pittsburgh.

As a thirty-five year veteran of the screen and digital printing industry, he leads research and development for Dprint and is the ultimate "Can Do!" resource for the company and its thousands of clients.

dprintworldwide.com | myDprint.com

Dprint CAPABILITIES

Certifications
- WBE by the State of Florida Office of Supplier Diversity
- SBA WOSB
- SGP Green-certified Production Facility
- WBE by WBENC
- DBE (pending)

NAICS
- 313310 Banners
- 323111 Digital Printing
- 323113 Screen Printing
- 541430 Graphic Design Services
- 541850 Outdoor Advertising
- (SIC 2759 Commercial Printing)

Contracts Sought
- Complex Decals and Static Cling
- Multi-part Wheels and Guides
- Parking Stickers/Hangtags
- Specialty Tags of All Types
- Non-electric Signs of All Constructions
- Murals
- Displays
- Vehicle Wraps
- Posters

We have spoken of the trust and confidence I have for your staff, the quality of Douglass' work and the conviction that once Douglass comes on board through a government contract, the Douglass team effort far exceeds the contractual requirements to provide outstanding service in a timely manner to the government.

We have worked with Dprint - formerly Douglass Screen Printers – for over 15 years now. Our expectations on quality and customer service continue to be exceeded for all of our needs. They provide dependable products and service second to none. I would highly recommend Dprint if you're looking for a company that can provide the Can Do attitude and results with a smile."

- Jeff Hile, Fleet Resources Manager, Saddle Creek Corporation

Core Capabilities
- Screen Printing
- Digital Printing - Flatbed, Web, Dye-Sublimation, Thermal
- Consecutive Numbering
- Hot/Cold Die Cutting
- Hot and Cold Lamination
- Routing
- Creative Design Services
- Digital Pre-press Automation
- Color Management
- Fabrication and Construction
- Packing/Shipping/Fulfillment Systems
- Installation

SAM (System for Award Management)
- We are registered and current on SAM.gov
- Our GPO contractor code is 090-28380
- We are registered with the SBA
- Our DUNS is 004110920

Performance History
- 57-year Member Specialty Graphic Imaging Association (SGIA)
- 35-year Unblemished Performance Record with USGPO
- Multiple Program Contractor with NASA, DOI (BLM) and DHS
- Multiple Awards Won for Diversity Practices, Corporate Social Responsibility, Printing and Innovation
- Contract Provider at $100,000+ Level to Departments of the Army, Navy, SSA, DHS and NASA

DEBORA CARRIGAN
GOVERNMENT ACCOUNTS
P. 863.899.7130
F. 863.582.9903
E. DCARRIGAN@myDprint.COM

Dprint
dprintworldwide.com

MORE CAPABILITIES STATEMENT EXAMPLES

ANDREINA PRADAS

How it is Delivered:
One-on-one and group sessions online or in-person; flexible to approach based upon needs assessed with the client.

Geographies:
North, Central, and South America; and Europe.

Industry Focus:
Healthcare, NGOs, Education, and Hospitality.

Certifications:
WBENC (Women's Business Enterprise)
WOSB (Women-Owned Small Business Federal Contract Program)

Contact:
URL: inhance.life
email: inhance@inhance.life
Telf.: (301) 633-2631

Key Clients:

inhance

Happiness Ambassador, Health Awareness & Wellness Educator, creator of the "3 Steps to Profitability Through Happiness" Program.

Company Name:
Andreina is the founder of Inhance where her mission is to help people who have lost their belief and faith in the life and companies they have created to reconnect to themselves, so they can find harmony again with everything they love.

With 85% of the workforce and 350 million people globally suffering depression and extreme stress from work responsibilities, Andreina's program provides companies the skills and resources to proactively manage this growing challenge in today's company cultures and to complement existing health and wellness support services already in place.

Core Competencies:
Andreina's productivity program, which she delivers globally with a specialized focus in Europe; North, Central and South American countries, "3 Steps to Profitability Through Happiness", is an innovative health awareness and wellness program she delivers to individuals and companies. She leads leadership and their employees on a concise path to reach their full potential, improve their relationships with others and increase productivity, building better teams and cultures with higher returns.

Certifications/Professional Affiliations:
Andreina is leveraging her background of more than 20 years of experience in human resources education working in the health, not-for-profit, hospitality and education fields. Andreina shares a proven systematic approach to help individuals find fulfillment and for companies to achieve higher productivity levels while not sacrificing the health of their employees.

Andreina has a Master's degree in Human Resource Development from George Washington University in Washington, DC and postgraduate studies from Harvard University and Cornell University. She is a 2012 Executive Leadership Program alumna from National Hispana Leadership Institute (NHLI) and a Certified Coach from the Newfield Network Program. She is a Senior Certified Professional by the Society for Human Resource Management (SCP-SHRM) and a member of the South Florida Hispanic Chamber of Commerce Business Committee.

IT Equipment, Solutions and Services

Women's Business Enterprise
National Council

Billie Bryant

Founding Member

Board of Directors
Their Women Client Committee
Presented March 5, 1999

About CESCO

We are a strong 54 year old company that provides excellent customer service, cost savings and innovative technologies to our valued clients.

Our Services

- Sales & Leasing of IT Equipment
- Managed Print Services
- Assessment of IT Projects
- Project Management
- Optimization
- Device Deployment & Training
- Data Protection & Secure Printing
- On-Site Repair
- EDI Billing

Our Products

- Copiers, Multifunctional Devices, Printers, 3D printers
- Printer Software Solutions
- Toner - OEM & Remanufactured
- Servers, Desktops, Laptops, Chromebooks & Tablets
- Mailing & Shipping Equipment
- Data Protection & Management

General Information

CESCO, Inc.
CEO, Billie Bryant Schultz

Certified Women's Business Enterprise
Certified Woman-Owned Small Business
Certified Disadvantaged Business Enterprise
NCTRCA
Certified Texas HUB

Contact Information

bbryant@cesco-inc.com
(214) 824-8741
www.cesco-inc.com

Community Involvement

For the past three years CESCO has designed, delivered, and sponsored young girls at Harmony Schools in Dallas to attend the Go for the Greens Women's Conference in Orlando, Florida.

11969 PLANO ROAD SUITE 130, DALLAS, TX 75243 • (214) 824-8741 • (800) 346-2685

● TIP #11

PERFECT YOUR PITCH

When you approach a potential customer or client to talk about what your business does and how you do it, you are making a "pitch." This is your opportunity to make a meaningful impression and get a conversation started. It's essential that you get off on the right foot, no matter what kind of business you have or who you're approaching.

A good pitch has a good rhythm and is easy to remember — both for you and for the person on the receiving end. Keep in mind that the key is to make it your own. Your pitch has to be in your voice.

> 66
>
> *Building a brand means knowing your story and building and sharing that story.*
>
> — Tamara McCleary
>
> 99

Every good pitch has some key elements:

- **Who you are.** Start your pitch with information about your company. Include years in business, years of experience, number of employees and, if possible, revenue over the past three to five years. One of our clients always points out that she was the first person to get WBENC-certified in Florida. This shows her company's trailblazing, longevity, and continued success since she keeps recertifying.

- **What you do.** Be specific. Don't hesitate to brag. Be sure to present innovative products or services your company offers. Don't be afraid to drop names of competitors of the company you're pitching to if you are doing business with them. This will be translated into the fact that you know the industry and you will be able to hit the ground running because you have experience and expertise in the field.

- **Your audience.** Keep in mind who you are talking to and adapt your pitch to those individuals. It's OK to do some name dropping. Talk about your experience with companies like theirs.

- **How you do it.** Talk about your team. Present solutions that are common in their industry. If you keep getting the same questions about your product or service, include those and the answers in your pitch.

- **Why you do it.** Talk about your purpose and your mission. What unique perspective do you bring to your projects? Simon Sinek gives great ideas about this in the book *Start with Why: How Great Leaders Inspire Everyone to Take Action* and his TED Talk by the same name.

- **Your experience:** Cover the number of years your company has been in business and showcase your expert status. If your company is new (under 3 years old) use that to your advantage: state that you started your business to bring innovative ideas to the industry. Emphasize the number of years of experience you brought to your business.

Keep in mind that your pitch should be two to four minutes. If you make it longer than four minutes, you might lose their attention. Make sure to practice. Your pitch must flow and sound natural. And finally, adapt and adopt. You can use one of several different versions of your pitch, varying the context and length depending on your audience.

❯ TIP #12

LEVERAGE YOUR PROFESSIONAL PROFILE ON LINKEDIN

If you are like most small business owners, you've been running your business and not paying too much attention to your LinkedIn profile and pages. Too many people think of LinkedIn as the place to go to get a job. It is that, but it's so much more.

For business owners, a solid LinkedIn presence can help you target new clients and get the lowdown on your competitors. Publishing content on LinkedIn can give you expert status to make you and your business stand out.

> 66
>
> *Lean in, speak out, have a voice in your organization, and never use the word 'sorry.'*
>
> — Trish Bertuzzi
>
> 99

Ten things you can and should do to make the most of your LinkedIn profile and improve your visibility:

1. **Update your photo.** Your photo is the first thing people see when they look at your profile. If it's more than five years old, get a new one. If you don't have a professional headshot, now is the time.

2. **Join groups.** Be strategic when selecting groups. Which groups can you count on for industry expertise, thought leadership, innovation and creativity? Don't forget your college alumni groups. And once you're in, be sure to comment and share articles and posts.

3. **Update your skills list.** This one should be pretty obvious, but so

---

RESOURCE

Do you want to do business with a particular company? Look it up on LinkedIn. Comment on the company's posts. Follow the same groups the company follows. When you meet people from that company, this gives you a perfect way to connect because you can talk about what is important to them.

many people fail to keep their skills list updated. Take a close look at the work you do for your top clients. Are those skills highlighted in your profile?

4. **Use multimedia to your advantage.** In case you didn't know this, you can link all sorts of things to your profile pages, including videos, PowerPoint or SlideShare presentations, photos of your events and pictures of your awards and accomplishments.

5. **Look at your recommendations.** How old are they? Ask current

RESOURCE
Use videos. Record a supply chain process. Record a how-to-process about your product or service. Keep the recordings to less than three minutes.

clients to write recommendations. Better yet, take something they said, craft it into a recommendation and ask them to do you a favor and post it. Offer to return the favor.

6. **Review your LinkedIn URL.** First name/last name usually does the trick. If you have a common name as I do, add a middle name or industry marker — for example NancyAllenSpeaker or NancyAllenCoach.

7. **Rethink your title.** LinkedIn defaults to your current job title. You can change that and make it more appealing: "Creator of _____." "Author of _____."

8. **Follow the right people.** Make sure you stay on top of industry leaders. Is there anyone new in the space? Any new publications? Track down the industry experts, and don't forget to follow corporations you are targeting as clients.

9. **Expand your profile.** Fill out the additional categories. Do you

volunteer in your community or support particular causes? Information like this adds gravitas and color to your profile.

10. **Be intentional about posting.** At least have a plan in mind when reposting, sharing and commenting on other people's relevant posts. They will greatly appreciate it, and you will stand out. For example, you can write: "What a great article. Thanks for the insight. My takeaways are (1), (2), (3)."

❯ TIP #13

NURTURE NEW LEADS

Want to nurture new leads without inundating people's inboxes? Consider sending one email a week for 12 weeks. People do business with the people they know, like and trust, right? Create an intentional campaign that accomplishes all three.

How to get people to know you:

- **Tell your story!** Consider doing a video or interview series about why you started your company.

- **Highlight your staff.** Who has been with you the longest? Who is the newest member of your team?

- **Talk about milestones.** Recognize anniversaries, the number of clients, new clients, new offices, new products or services.

- **List 10 things people don't know about you.** Do you play an instrument? Were you in the Girl Scouts? Where have you traveled? Do you love to cook, garden or read?

> *I realized that if I was willing to step up and be in the spotlight, I'd be able to make everyone else around me much more powerful as well.*
>
> — Alaina Percival

How to get people to like you:

- **Show how you give back.** Do you have a favorite charity? Consider starting a business tradition of helping out in your community and invite your clients to join in. Our most successful members are very committed to supporting their local communities. They give their employees time off to participate in community activities like youth athletic leagues, Boy Scout and Girl Scout activities, local food banks and other causes. Include your "give back" policy on your website and in your marketing materials. It will go a long way toward showing current and potential clients that you support your local community.

- **Launch a social media campaign.** Hold a contest to increase the "likes" to your pages.

- **Network and make connections.** Make the networking meetings you attend intentionally about connecting people who should know each other.

- **Recommend and endorse.** Interact with people and companies on LinkedIn, Yelp and other social media channels.

How to get people to trust you:

- **List and update your clients on your website.** Ask their permission to use their logos and/or their names.

- **Use testimonials.** Don't be afraid to ask for testimonials. You can make it easy to get testimonials by drafting them yourself and then asking for permission to post them on your website. For instance, if clients have told you they are happy with your product or service, use their own words to draft the testimonial. Offer to provide a link to their website from yours.

- **Be a thought leader**. Blog, write articles, get quoted in local and national publications. Offer to provide insight and background to newspapers and local media.

- **Highlight your awards.** This isn't bragging, it's informing your existing and potential clients that you are well regarded and celebrated for your achievements.

Not comfortable doing this in three months? How about a 12-month campaign where you highlight one thing every month? After all, you know what they say about marketing: It takes many touches and in different modalities to get noticed.

❯ TIP #14

STORYTELLING AS A FORM OF MARKETING

You've probably heard that people remember stories more than they remember straight facts and statistics. Storytelling is a powerful tool to connect with others. So, why not use it in your marketing?

Large corporations do this all the time. Think about the most successful commercials and ad campaigns. Those are (very) short stories intended to pull you in and make a point. Social media has made storytelling easy, compelling and, some would argue, mandatory from a marketing standpoint. Even if you don't consider yourself a good storyteller, you can still use stories to set you and your company apart.

> " *We need to accept that we won't always make the right decisions, that we'll screw up royally sometimes – understanding that failure is not the opposite of success, it's part of success.*
>
> — Arianna Huffington "

You can use storytelling for these purposes:

- Increase sales
- Generate leads
- Educate consumers
- Persuade people to change their behavior
- Inform and train
- Highlight your success
- Showcase your clients
- Motivate your employees

A good story has some essential elements. To tell a good story, you need to know who, what, where, when and how. In other words:

- **Characters.** Good stories often have a hero or main character that readers can connect to emotionally.

- **Setting.** Where does the story take place?

- **Plot.** There should be an order of events in the story.

- **Point of view.** The way you see the story, and why, are important.

- **Conflict.** What happens when the main character encounters obstacles? As a business owner, you must have faced many obstacles that you were able to overcome. One of our members tells how she went a couple of weeks without pay, surviving on peanut butter sandwiches, so she could keep her staff in place. She bet on a very large contract coming through that got delayed. Her perseverance kept her business open, and her sacrifice translated to very loyal employees who appreciated knowing that they were valued so much.

- **Resolution.** What happens when your characters achieve their goals? What do they learn and how do they change? Good storytellers open and close loops. Don't forget to do that when you tell a story, too. And it's always a good idea to spell out the point of your story after you share it with the audience. This serves to reinforce your points.

- **Theme.** What are the big ideas the story is supposed to convey? It's also a good idea to weave your personal and business core values into your stories. As a matter of fact, you might be able to find stories to develop just by looking at your core values. You can develop stories related to how you honored or bumped up against your core values.

Your story doesn't have to be very long to be impactful. It does have to be truthful, and it does have to be authentic to your brand and market. Here's an example:

For years I told the following story as a way to get people to remember the name of my company and what I do. When my son was in kindergarten, his class had a career day. The teacher asked each student what his or her daddy did for a living. Then she asked each student, "How does your mommy spend her day?" Keep in mind, this was more than 20 years ago, and most of the children's mothers were stay-at-home moms.

My son answered the first question by saying his dad was a periodontist, and he explained to the class that this is a kind of dentist who gives people new permanent teeth. When asked the second question, Mark looked up and thought about it. He couldn't remember that I worked at the Women's Business Development Council of Florida, so he said: "My mommy spends her day in the company of women." Well, there you have it. From the mouths of babes! I do get to spend my day in the company of women because I work with women business owners who want to access corporate and federal contracts.

I can't tell you how many people would see me at different meetings and say, "Oh yes, you're the person who works in the company of women!" Instant icebreaker and relatable story.

What is your story?

Here are five stories you and your team can share:

1. How you landed your first client.

2. The story behind your company logo.

3. The story behind your company name.

4. Stories about your employees. Have they been with you from the start of your business? One person I know always mentions that she has three generations of employees from the same family working at her company. This speaks to loyalty, to business longevity, and to their core values.

5. Stories about special causes you support and why.

► TIP #15

CREATE POWERFUL PRESENTATIONS

To help promote your business and continue to build your reputation as an expert, you'll want to find opportunities to speak in public or participate in panel discussions or group presentations. These are great opportunities to help you stand out — if you take full advantage of them and do them right. Giving a compelling presentation is easier than you think.

> "
>
> *Growth and comfort do not coexist.*
>
> — Ginni Rometty
>
> "

Ten elements of delivering a talk that will keep your audience buzzing long after the event:

1. **Know your audience.** Ask for background information on your audience, such as:
   - Age
   - Gender
   - Number of participants
   - Why they are there

> **RESOURCE**
> One of our members uses a speaker information sheet. She sends this questionnaire out before accepting a speaking engagement. It helps to set and manage expectations, and it helps her prepare the right presentation for each audience.

2. **Passion and connection.** Be enthusiastic! Let audience members know you can help them. Ask for feedback and participation along the way.
   - "Is this making sense to you?"
   - "Raise your hand if you agree."

3. **Them, not you.** Focus on their needs.
- What's in it for them?
- What can they learn?
- What will they remember?

4. **Simple and concise.** Pay attention to the time.
- Use 10 to 15 slides maximum.
- Take 20 minutes maximum.
- Allow time for questions and answers.

5. **Mix it up!** Use different media to make your points.
- Photos
- Video clips
- Charts and infographics

6. **Make eye contact and smile.** Establish a physical connection.
- Practice your body language.
- Scan the room to connect with your audience.
- Use your hands to make a point.

7. **Use storytelling.** Everyone remembers a good tale.
- Every good story has a beginning, a middle and an end.
- Weave the story throughout your presentation.
- My storytelling coach says every story should have a point and every point should have a story.

8. **Focus on communication.** What does your voice sound like?
   - Practice.
   - Practice.
   - Practice.
   - Don't read or memorize your presentation.

9. **Start sharp and end strong.** Let your audience know what you will tell them.
   - Tell them — and give them great information.
   - Ask whether you delivered.

10. **Remember a call to action.** What's next for them and you?
    - Be specific.
    - Be proactive.
    - Give them something to do immediately.

NOTES

_____

_____

_____

_____

_____

_____

_____

_____

► TIP #16

GROW YOUR BUSINESS WITH STRATEGIC ALLIANCES

Have you ever been in a position of not being able to bid on a contract because your company wasn't big enough or you didn't have some of the expertise you needed in-house? This can be frustrating for small business owners and can keep you from growing because of the extra costs and time involved in researching how you can fill in the gaps. Sometimes you can solve this issue by entering into a strategic alliance.

> " Don't be intimidated by what you don't know. That can be your greatest strength and ensure that you do things differently from everyone else.
>
> — Sara Blakely

At its most basic, a strategic alliance is a partnership of two or more companies with a common goal centered around growth and development. Strategic alliances can take on many different forms. Some collaborations operate under a joint venture agreement and have formal organizational documents to spell out the details. Other alliances involve a large prime supplier partnered with a smaller diverse supplier that together propose to provide a solution in a rather informal agreement. Sometimes a smaller diverse supplier comes in as a prime and partners with a larger supplier as one of its subcontractors.

One of our members was considering bidding on a contract with her local school district. She was already a supplier for the district, but this contract was in a different area of expertise than the customer was used to her company handling. She wasn't sure her company's bid would be taken seriously. She decided to call in two other diverse suppliers whose companies specialized in areas that were not core capabilities of her company — one of the suppliers was another WBENC member and the other was minority-owned. Together the three created a strategic alliance to go after the bid.

They approached the alliance as a business proposition. They discussed in advance which of their three companies would handle which part of the work if they received the bid. They decided how and when each of them would be compensated. They worked out a system of how they would manage the project and stay in communication with each other — and who would be the point person with the client on each part of the project. They got the bid.

You should consider forming or joining a strategic alliance if you are not currently able to meet the demands of a contract on your own. Strategic alliances can serve to bridge the gap to help:

- Cover a certain geographical footprint.
- Create additional commercial capabilities.
- Bring stronger financial viability.

Strategic alliances have many benefits for both the businesses involved and for the corporations they are soliciting, including:

- Improved market reach.
- Generation of additional revenue.
- Development of new products, markets and skills.
- Risk management.
- Easier performance management.

What should you consider in forming a strategic alliance?

- Do your homework with the proposed customer to have the organization understand the joint venture you're considering. Make sure the customer is comfortable with what you're planning to do.

- Do your due diligence with the supplier or group of suppliers you are considering partnering with. Ensure they have skills and commercial requirements you are looking for before forming an alliance.

- This is a significant development opportunity. Although you may be sharing the opportunities, look at it for the long-term benefits of getting to know the client company and getting your foot in the door. Consider that some of the money from a particular contract is better than none of the money.

As you contemplate and develop a strategic alliance, be sure to keep the following things in mind:

- Take into account, outline and agree to an exit strategy before you sign on the dotted line.
- Create an official contract for the strategic alliance. Be very specific about payment expectations and terms. I know of several strategic alliances that came apart because of issues with payments and timing. Don't let that happen to you.
- Search for partners within and outside of your network and industry. You can find potential partners by attending pre-bid conferences and also by developing a relationship with procurement officers and supplier diversity managers. Let them know you're interested in establishing a strategic alliance and ask for recommendations.
- Decide which company will be the lead for interactions with the customer.
- Clearly define the roles of the parties involved.
- Outline and agree to everyone's expectations.
- Pick a partner with different strengths than yours.
- Define and agree to the market reach for the alliance: local, regional, national, international.
- Evaluate your cultural fit. Do the parties all have the same core values?
- Establish performance metrics: financial, strategic, operational. Consider and agree on what happens if performance metrics are not met by one or more parties.

The corporate partners and sponsors I've worked with at the Women's Business Enterprise Council of Florida have told me their purchasing departments and contract officers prefer to award contracts to businesses that form and promote that they are strategic alliances because they are efficient and because they offer creative and innovative solutions.

> **RESOURCE**
> Are you considering expanding overseas? Creating a strategic alliance with an established company in the market you're targeting would make a lot of sense. You can also promote the fact that you are successful in a market and offer to join forces with someone interested in expanding to your location.

NOTES

_____

_____

_____

_____

_____

_____

_____

_____

_____

○ TIP #17

GET THE MOST OUT OF ATTENDING CONFERENCES

One sure way to make new contacts and learn more about how to be a better leader for your company is to attend conferences where you can network with peers and meet potential customers. Instead of just showing up, however, there are ways to get the most out of the event.

Make the investment of your time and money a success by preparing before, actively participating during, and keeping engaged after. Conferences can be overwhelming, so here are some pre-, during- and post-conference strategies to help you get the most out of the experience.

> "
> *I got lucky because I never gave up the search. Are you quitting too soon? Or are you willing to pursue luck with a vengeance too?*
> — Jill Konrath
> "

Pre-conference

- **Update your capabilities statement and stock up on business cards.** You'll need these tools to be sure you leave a good impression and a reminder with important people you meet. My advice is that you do not spend a lot of money on multiple copies of brochures or bound project information that you expect to leave behind. Would you carry dozens or hundreds of people's papers back on the plane with you? Instead, create a slick one-of-a-kind business card that helps you stand out from the crowd and be memorable. Create just a few bound copies of your presentation that you can show, and then offer to send it along electronically if needed.

- **Do your homework.** Visit the conference website and identify the major sponsors. Are they on your target list?

- **Identify five prospects.** Determine what you could bring to them and how you can offer your products or services to them. Prepare to find a way to meet with them.

- **Consider reaching out to target companies in advance.** Be purposeful. Connect with them on LinkedIn or Twitter. Send your capabilities statement and links to your website, and let the contacts know you look forward to seeing them at the event.

- **Pre-register on the websites of your target companies.** Go to the supplier diversity portals and register as a vendor. Be sure to update your information if you've previously registered.

- **Decide on your expected outcome.** Who do you want to connect with? How many workshops do you want to attend? Who will you visit during the business expo? Be sure to register as a supplier or vendor on the website of your target corporations.

- **Double check all conference deadlines.** For example, eligibility for matchmaker meetings at the Women's Business Enterprise National Council conferences requires that you register for the full conference before the early bird deadline. Book your hotel early. If possible, stay at the host hotel. Transportation is easier, and there are always lots of networking opportunities in the hotel lobby or bar area.

- **Organize and participate in pre-conference meetups.** Get to know people who are attending the conference and get the camaraderie going.

- **Download the conference app and complete your profile.** This makes it easy for people to find you during and after the event.

- **Download or print out the exhibit hall map.** Familiarize yourself with the map of the venue and schedule of events on the conference website. Study the locations of the corporations you want to visit at a tradeshow. Be strategic with your time.

During the conference

- **Wear your name badge at all times.** Shorten the lanyard so people can easily see your name. This helps you avoid the awkward moment when someone can't remember your name and has to steal glimpses at your belly.

- **Attend the workshops and ask questions.** Always state your name and company name when you step up to the microphone. Thank the speaker or panelists for the great information and then ask your question. Consider thinking of questions and writing them down ahead of time so you're prepared when the Q&A portion starts.

- **Use the conference hashtag.** Take photos during the event and post them along with positive comments on social media.

- **Introduce yourself.** People expect that. Be a connector and introduce and welcome people to your group.

- **Make allies and believers.** Focus on relationship building. People do business with people they know, like and trust. Offer to make introductions or give referrals, and ask people to do the same for you. Set yourself up as a great resource and solutions provider.

- **Wear comfortable shoes and layers for temperature changes.** I can't stress that enough. No one can look and feel her best when all she can think about is how uncomfortable her shoes are or how she's freezing. Bring a shawl or a sweater.

Post-conference

- **Write thank you notes.** A handwritten note is best. This will set you apart because most people will send emails. An envelope will be opened more readily than an email. Who should you thank? Conference organizers, conference sponsors, workshop panelists, guest speakers and anyone else who helps you. Besides showing good manners, a thank you note gives you an opportunity for branding. Use a note card with your logo. Tell speakers how inspiring they were. Post your comments on their social media.

- **Ask the contacts you made if you can put them on your mailing list.** This is a good way for you to stay in touch with each other.

- **Get onto LinkedIn later and connect with everyone you met.** Again, this is a great way to stay in touch and expand each of your networks. Sometimes you might even want to connect together on the spot.

- **Establish a follow-up calendar for people you met who might be good leads.** Are you an author? Send them a copy of your book. Consider sending books or magazines on relevant topics to people you want to connect with. Nurturing relationships is key to building trust and remaining top of mind.

- **Celebrate your accomplishments at the conference.** Did you meet your outreach goals? Did you have a successful matchmaker meeting? Gain some insight that might open new markets or opportunities? Meet someone who might be a good candidate for a strategic alliance? Smile because you made progress!

Notice I did not say celebrate a new contract? That very rarely happens. You don't usually leave a conference with immediate contracts. Conferences are for building relationships and for showcasing your talents and expertise. Be a resource. Be a connector and be open to opportunity, but don't judge yourself poorly if you don't see immediate results.

▶ TIP #18

MASTER THE ART OF THE FOLLOW-UP

So you just got back from a conference or networking event, and you're excited about the connections you made. Now what?

Don't get lost in the land of overwhelm and procrastination. Apply the following tips and watch your contacts grow into connections and contracts. Here is what you need to do:

> *The most successful entrepreneurs I know are optimistic. It's part of the job description.*
> — Caterina Fake

Sort through your new contacts

Not all of the people you met will require the same type of attention. To help you determine which contacts need which action steps, organize the business cards you've gathered into three piles.

- Pile 1: Follow up with answers to questions they asked when you met.
- Pile 2: Follow up with potential resources so you can further your relationship with them.
- Pile 3: Put them into your general mailing list.

Once you finish, send a handwritten thank you note to the people in Piles 1 and 2. A handwritten note is memorable and sets you apart. Most importantly, it shows that you are committed to the relationship. Be sure to customize your notes with your address and contact information.

Next, connect with all of your new contacts on LinkedIn and other social media channels.

Finally, enter the business cards into a database.

Create a follow-up system

Do your homework on the company and the company representatives.
- What is the best way to communicate with them? Sign up for their mailing lists, and join industry groups they're in.
- Do your prospects have your current capabilities statement? If not, then send it to them.
- Do your prospects know you are interested in first-tier and second-tier opportunities?

Set contact goals

It is essential to set outreach goals and to stick to them.
- Establish a calendar system for keeping in contact. Remember it can take up to seven touches to make an impression. Be creative in how you provide them.
- Determine how you will keep in contact. Email? Phone calls? Meetings?
- Determine how often you will keep in contact. Monthly? Quarterly? Annually?
- People do business with people they know, like and they trust. Everything starts with a relationship.

Here are some examples of how you can build a stable relationship:

- **Be a resource!** Make sure your prospects identify you as someone who is a resource. Remember they think in terms of W.I.F.M. (What's in it for me?) Reach out to them with information and referrals at first. Don't just focus on WIFM from your perspective.

- **Maintain contact.** The best way to establish a relationship is by staying in touch so you can be top-of-mind. Keep up to date on what is going on in the prospects' fields. Show your interest and help them look good. Join industry-specific networking groups.

- **Re-evaluate your goals.** Make sure you keep your prospects up to date on what's going on with your business. Make sure you and your prospect are still aligned. Determine whether you want to continue to pursue the relationship.

The key is to follow up. Luck is where opportunity meets preparation. Remember that it can take as long as three years for a contact to turn into a contract. Don't be discouraged. Stay in touch with the prospect using the tips above and you will be remembered and called when the time is right.

NURTURE RELATIONSHIPS WITH CORPORATE BUYERS

Women are known as being excellent at establishing and nurturing relationships. You can use the same natural skills you bring to the table with family, friends, colleagues and team members to build your relationships with buyers.

One of our members forged a relationship with IBM when her business was in its early years. Today, after almost three decades, the relationship is still thriving. Her company originally offered one core type of service, and over the years its portfolio has grown to include an expansive list of capabilities and a global reach. The company's champions at IBM have been there helping her company grow by challenging it to meet additional needs at the corporation. She calls IBM a core customer and collaborator, saying the two entities bring clients to one another and increase their complementary value proposition, jointly delivering innovative services to companies around the globe.

> *You will be defined not just by what you achieve, but by how you survive.*
>
> — Sheryl Sandberg

People often ask me about the best way to approach a corporation for a contract. The answer is simple: Speak the company's language and offer a solution it can use. Yes, it's that simple and also that hard.

Every corporation has its own language and its own culture. Just as Spanish is not the same language in every Spanish-speaking country — there are nuances and regionalisms — each industry and each corporation has variances that are very important to them. Here are a few tips to help you know you're speaking the right language:

- **Go to the company's website.** Read the About Us section and look for core values and vision and mission statements.
- **Read its annual reports.** Does the company refer to its employees as *team members* or by another title? Does it have supplier diversity *programs* or supplier diversity initiatives? Does it buy from *vendors* or *suppliers*?

- **Check out the company on social media.** What words does the organization use? Are its posts humorous, or are they formal? Does the company tell stories or stick to the facts?
- **Once you know the language, mirror it.** The easiest way to build rapport is to share a common language and cultural values. Your capabilities statement will resonate more with your prospects if it looks and feels familiar to them.

Let's be clear: I'm not suggesting that you stifle your personality, brand or culture. Instead, I'm suggesting that you understand theirs and present yourself as a potential partner with a dynamic solution to one of the company's everyday problems.

Your solution has to be financially feasible, it has to be easy to understand and replicate, and it has to make the corporate person presenting it look smart and innovative. One corporate representative explained to me that if he were a small business owner, he could make a contract decision based on a gut reaction, but as a corporate buyer he has to justify his decisions to his team — and beyond his team to the division — and beyond that to the executive vice president of purchasing. That's three layers of decision-makers. Can your product or service solution hold up to three layers or levels of scrutiny?

So, how good is your corporate-speak? Here are eight proven ways to get noticed by corporate buyers:

1. Do your homework.

- **Know what the company stands for and what it sells.** This is very easy to do because you can find information on the company's website and on social media.
- **Be mindful of the look and feel of the company.** If it is a conservative organization, mirror that branding with an approach that will appeal to the company. An edgy approach might not go over well with a conservative company, and a conservative approach will fizzle with an edgy company.
- **Use the organization's words and terminology.** This will serve you well as you develop a relationship with its representatives.
- **Sign up for the company's newsletters and media blasts.** This will keep you current on news the organization thinks is essential.

2. Provide solutions.

- **Mind how you present your product or service.** Be a solutions provider, not a contract seeker. What can you do for the company?
- **Tout your expertise.** What can you and your company bring that will save the organization money or time, help it gain market share, or accomplish one of its other goals?
- **Cite examples.** Talk about what you have done for others in similar industries. If possible, do some name-dropping of clients you work with and how you were able to help those clients.
- **Offer to be a speaker or trainer.** Don't wait to be asked — offer yourself up as a speaker, panelist or moderator at one of the corporation's events. Many corporations have affinity groups that meet regularly and often look for speakers and trainers. Offer your services to those groups because they often include a cross-section of employees and management.

3. Customize your pitch.

- **Keep it brief.** When you first meet corporate buyers, you have about 60 seconds to get and capture their attention. Can you articulate who you are and what you can do for someone in one minute?
- **Try a "teaser pitch."** If your business model or industry is technical or difficult to explain in 60 seconds, then you should develop a brief pitch that will intrigue your listener.
- **Customize your one-page capabilities statement.** Develop it to meet that corporation's needs. Limit it to one page, even if it is two-sided — this is a place where less is more. It should have a good-quality photo and should include your contact information as well as a client list.

4. Beef up your business description.

- **List awards and recognition.** Include the name of each honor and the year you received it.
- **Claim expert status in your industry.** Have you written any case studies or white papers on your product or service? Have you received any awards?
- **Say how your company is different.** Can you claim to be "the first" or "the only"? Do you have a network of independent contractors you can call on in different areas? This will show that your reach is more than regional or local. One of our members set up alliances with businesses similar to hers across the United States. When bidding for national contracts, she is able to say, "We have people in the areas you are targeting who live and work there. They know the area and will cut down on start-up or design time."

5. Examine your online presence.

- **Look at your web presence through their eyes.** Do your social media and your website both represent your business and look professional? You can actually lose a contract because your website does not look up to date or professional. I have been told time and time again that someone did not get a contract because buyers were not impressed with their website.
- **Keep your website up-to-date.** Does it look modern and accurately reflect what your company offers today, or does it need an update? Do you have easy-to-find testimonials? Do you have a client list? Does your business have a national or global reach? State that clearly and give examples or proof through testimonials and client names.
- **Keep the navigation simple.** Is your "Contact Us" section easy to find, and does it provide the information people need to reach you? Make it as easy as possible to find information and make the answers to their questions readily available so that visitors to your online network have a pleasant experience.

6. Use social media to enhance your brand.

- **Be sure to use social media appropriately.** Consider having a social media policy so anyone working with your social media will keep the branding consistent.
- **Understand the tools.** What you post on your company Facebook page is different than what goes on your company LinkedIn page, and those are different than what you'd post on Twitter.
- **Know your target audiences.** You should be aware of who each segment of social media is trying to attract and where to find those audience members.
- **Form and leverage strategic alliances.** Corporations would rather work with one small vendor than with 20. Are there other small businesses in your network that you can work with in a partnership, and can you co-brand on social media?

7. Be everywhere your buyers go.

- **Show up!** Being present at places and times where opportunities are available is half the battle.
- **Seek out corporate contacts at events.** Attend events where you know they will be. Make it a point to speak with them. The more they see you, the faster and better they'll get to know you.
- **Be a strategic networker.** Ask for introductions and be prepared to be the one making the introductions.

8. Follow up.

- **If appropriate, send them a handwritten thank you.** There is a fine line between being persistent and being a pest. Don't cross that line! Never send a second email with the subject line "This is the second email." And never reprimand the recipient for not giving you "the courtesy of a reply." Assume that the people you're approaching are busy and that they might not have opened your previous email. Use subject lines that will get them to open a new email instead of forwarding your previous emails.

- **Connect on LinkedIn.** Do this the day you meet someone or the next day — that's when you will be freshest in that person's mind.
- **Join online groups the buyers have joined.** Find out what groups they follow that you have in common, or join groups you are interested in that they are a part of already.
- **Follow their social media.** Get involved with their company social media presence and get a pulse on what's going on so you can be relevant and find opportunities to bring solutions to the table.

There are so many ways to build relationships with buyers, but it's about doing it naturally and authentically. This will take time and depends on your networking and branding. You can accelerate the efforts by finding mutual connections and common ground.

NOTES

_____

_____

_____

_____

_____

_____

_____

_____

Are you getting ready for an interview with a corporate contact? Here are seven tips to make sure you make a great impression:

1. Be on time. Arrive at least 15 minutes early so you have time to go to the bathroom to freshen up. Announce yourself clearly to the receptionist: "I'm _____." I have a 10 a.m. appointment with Mr./Mrs./Ms. _____."

2. Dress for success. Your outfit should match the corporate culture. When in doubt, men should wear a suit and tie, and women should wear a dress or skirt and blouse. Your shoes should be clean. Make sure your hair is well-groomed.

3. Make a good first impression. The interview starts in the parking lot. Be courteous to everyone you meet. Watch your body language. Be open and enthusiastic. Greet the interviewer with a handshake and a smile.

4. Be ready when someone says, "Tell me about yourself." Craft a compelling narrative that describes you and your business. Emphasize your accomplishments, and make sure you relate those to the potential contract at hand.

5. Ask insightful questions. Be prepared with some questions to ask the person interviewing you, such as, "What are you looking for in a vendor?" "What is the timeframe for making a decision?" "How do you like to be contacted during the process?"

6. End on a positive note. Say, "Thank you for your time." Ask for the business: "I am very interested in working with you." Say something positive such as, "I am confident that I can do this work, and I look forward to hearing from you." Offer additional information, such as "I am happy to provide references if that will help your decision."

7. Follow up. Send a handwritten note of thanks. Ask for feedback if you do not get chosen for the work. Don't burn any bridges.

► TIP #20

SAY THANK YOU

Close your eyes for a minute. Think back on the last time you received a snail-mail thank you card. If you're like me, you're smiling at the memory. I am so grateful when I receive a thank you note — for gifts, for advice I've given, for introductions, for helping someone through a rough patch, and for things I didn't even know I did at the time. My heart smiles at the gesture — and I can't quite put my finger on why, but it feels different when people intentionally set aside time to share their appreciation.

> Appreciation can make a day – even change a life. Your willingness to put it into words is all that is necessary.
>
> — Margaret Cousins

You can send notes to colleagues, employees, clients and random people who've done something that you find remarkable. Do this and watch the magic happen. You will feel good, they will feel good, and gratitude spreads like wildfire.

Send thank you notes to people who:
- Have been doing business with you for a long time.
- Just started doing business with you.
- Referred your services or products to others.
- You consider "engines."
- Make it possible for you to do what you do because it always takes teamwork.

Keep in mind that the best thank you notes have three characteristics:
1. **They are specific:** Be sure to mention the particular thing you are grateful for, or how and where you met.
2. **They are succinct:** Enough words to connect the dots and (hopefully!) make the person smile. Less is more and also more memorable.
3. **They are personal:** Let your personality and your style come through. Find unique stationery that you only use for this purpose or get a fun pen. Do whatever it takes for you to look forward to writing these, and to feel proud of your notes when you do send them out.

You might be saying, "But Nancy, my chicken scratch is illegible." Handwritten notes are best. So slow down, practice mindfulness, feel your gratitude and let it spill out on the paper. If you do that, your handwriting will be perfectly legible to your reader. Use words like *generous, generosity, useful, helpful, perfect, thoughtful, appreciate, grateful, much needed, always* and *treasure.*

Phrases that show gratitude and appreciation:
- I appreciate what you did.
- You made it possible for me to...
- You're the best! You are always x, y, z for me, and I want you to know I appreciate that...
- I'm wearing the smile you gave me.
- I'm humbled and grateful.
- I'm touched beyond words.
- I'm touched by your gesture.
- Your kindness is touching.
- Your thoughtfulness is a gift I will treasure.
- I appreciate your kindness.
- You went above and beyond, and I am grateful.
- Thanks for all your help.
- I owe you big time.
- You made it easier for me to...
- Thanks for being there.
- I'll never forget your kindness.
- Thank you for being my biggest supporter. I couldn't do it without you.

- I can't thank you enough, so please accept my flowers as a small token of my appreciation.
- I am so grateful for all you do; I can't thank you enough.
- Thanks for your patience, your loving words, your kindness, your friendship.
- When the whole world left, you were there with open arms. Thank you for being a true friend!
- You were there for me when I needed you the most! Thank you for your support. I truly appreciate it.

Thank you notes also have six necessary components:

1. **Greeting or salutation.** This is the greeting at the beginning of the note. Rule of thumb: If this is your first correspondence, be more formal than informal.
2. **Your real, true, authentic reason for writing.** This should be in the first few sentences. Be succinct.
3. **Be sure to make it personal.** Remind the person how and where you met. Mention the specific occasion.
4. **Strive to establish a connection.** Open the possibility of reaching out again.
5. **Be enthusiastic.** Have a positive tone throughout.
6. **Sign-off or valediction.** This is the closing at the end of the note. Again, if this is your first correspondence, make it warm but more formal, such as "With appreciation."

Mastering the art of thank you notes is not rocket science. The impact they make can be the start of a relationship that will be mutually beneficial. Remember that there have to be about seven marketing touches before someone starts to notice you, so make one of those touches a sincere thank you.

EMBRACE THE POWER OF DELEGATING

I once coached a small business owner whose business had grown tremendously over a year and then began to stagnate. She called me when the company was on the verge of decline. She couldn't understand what happened. She was doing the same marketing, and had an excellent reputation and the blessing of referral-based business. I sensed the problem as soon as I met her, after three canceled meetings on her end, and confirmed the issue after a short conversation. She was doing everything herself. That was important when she started the business but now, almost two years in, it was not possible anymore.

> *Trying to do it all and expecting it all can be done exactly right is a recipe for disappointment. Perfection is the enemy.*
>
> — Sheryl Sandberg

Why are we so resistant to delegating? Is it control, perfectionism, fear? It's probably a combination of the three and a little more like an aversion to making the time to set up policies and procedures formally.

I say if you are not delegating, you are not growing. And if you're not growing, your business won't either.

Four reasons you should consider delegating some of your tasks:

1. **Focus on priorities.** Delegating will give you more time to concentrate *on* your business rather than working *in* your business.
2. **Team development.** Delegating will help you get more buy-in from your team. When you delegate, you show your employees that you trust them. This goes a long way toward fostering commitment and job satisfaction.
3. **Better results.** Chances are your team members have strengths and specialized skills, and you should take advantage of them. Give them a way to shine and take advantage of the talent you already have.

4. **Fresh insight.** Delegating tasks and projects brings in new perspectives. We often do not see opportunities because we are so used to doing something one way that we don't allow the space for creativity.

It's time to delegate when:

- You feel that there is not enough time in the day and things are falling by the wayside.
- Your typical day and your ideal day don't match up.
- You're not spending enough time with your clients.
- You can tolerate different approaches to completing a task. You can't delegate and not give away some autonomy. You can set parameters and boundaries, but you have to let go some of the control.
- Your employees are already handling other projects by themselves and succeeding.
- Your employees have asked for more responsibility. Very often people let us know they can help and we ignore them. Why not have a conversation to determine whether they really can add value to the project?
- You know your employee could take over after a short training period.
- You trust your employee to respect the boundaries you set up.

If you are new at this, I suggest baby steps. Start small. Take time to evaluate your day and how you spend time. Read *The Big Leap: Conquer Your Hidden Fear and Take Life to the Next Level* by Dr. Gay Hendricks. Are you stuck doing things you don't have the skills and desire to do? Rest assured that there are people around you — or who would be easy to identify and access — who will probably relish doing those things.

The perfect team has all sorts of skill levels and interests. Concentrate on your strengths. Your business and your clients will be better for it. And that client I told you about earlier? She adopted the mantra, "I am letting go so I can grow." She hired an assistant and brought on two freelancers. It turned out she needed three people to handle everything that she was doing by herself. The results six months later were impressive: She moved into a larger space and hired one of the freelancers full-time.

What are you willing to let go so you can grow?

NOTES

_____

_____

_____

_____

_____

_____

_____

_____

_____

_____

_____

_____

_____

_____

_____

_____

SECTION 3
COMPANY
DEVELOPMENT

• GETTING READY

COMPANY DEVELOPMENT

S caling your company will take careful planning. It's not just a matter of bringing in more money. You need to have plans in place to handle a growing number of customers or clients, a larger number of projects and an expanding team. The planning will make the difference between whether you scale for growth the first time or have to stop, evaluate and try again.

If you're like most small business owners, the prospect of scaling can be overwhelming. The decision to scale will happen many times over the course of your business. You can make that decision less daunting and, over time, a natural next step if you take the time to put certain key elements of business development in place. Of course, you want to do more than just put them in place — you want to set metrics to monitor growth, keep you on track and help you with the decision to pivot when necessary.

This section talks about the different kinds of structure you'll need to have in place to begin this journey toward scaling. With plans that outline your intention, and then some other tools that help you guide your team and protect your assets, you will be well on your way to making your company larger and more profitable.

⊙ TIP #22

CRAFT A STRATEGIC PLAN

One of the most famous quotes from the late Dr. Stephen Covey was "Begin with the end in mind." This is the second habit laid out in his book *The 7 Habits of Highly Effective People.* I am a massive proponent of strategic planning because I sincerely believe that what gets planned gets done. Your strategic plan is the roadmap for your business. It illustrates:

> "
>
> *The backbone of success is hard work, determination, good planning and perseverance.*
>
> — Mia Hamm
>
> "

- Where you're going and how you are going to get there.
- The overarching goals and the part your employees play in the organization's success.

An effective strategic plan should contain these seven elements:

1) **Vision statement.** This should be ambitious and goal-oriented. It's a statement that looks at the overall direction of where it is you want your business to go. It's the "what" and "why" for everything you do.

2) **Mission statement.** This is about what's going on today: what you do, who you do it for and how you do it.

3) **Core values.** Your core values are those things you believe in that will enable you to achieve your vision and your mission. Some samples of core values include diversity (my favorite!), leadership, honesty, accountability and quality. You build and grow your business based on these values. It's important for your team to buy into and embrace these principles so you are all on the same page as the company grows.

4) **A SWOT analysis.** This is an exercise you will want to do a few times a year and throughout the life of your business. SWOT is an acronym that stands for strengths, weaknesses, opportunities and threats. The strengths and weaknesses come from an internal analysis. The opportunities and threats come from analyzing what's happening outside of your company. Look at what you're very good at and what sets you apart from your competition. What are the strengths and differentiators that you offer your target market? On the other side, study your weaknesses. Change your perspective and you might see that you can easily convert a weakness into a strength. A word of caution, though: A strength can also become a weakness if you're not careful about it.

5) **Long-term goals.** A lot of people start their businesses thinking, "OK, I'm going to get through the first year and the second year." They never really look beyond that first couple of years. To be successful in business, you have to look way beyond and envision the future you want. A good question to keep in mind as you craft your long-term goals is about legacy — what will your business legacy be?

6) **Yearly objectives.** Within the next three to five years, you want to break down your year by one-month increments and then take a look at your objectives. Even within those 12 months, I would suggest adding a milestone point biyearly to check in and see whether your company needs to make any course corrections. For example, let's say you started the year intending to make $1 million in revenue. By June, you should be halfway to your mark and trending toward obtaining it. At the milestone, revise either up or down, depending on the state of affairs.

7) **Action plan.** The final element of an excellent strategic plan is an action plan. Each objective should have details on how you will achieve and measure the goal. Who does what? When do they do it? How do they do it?

There are many examples and templates for creating a strategic plan. An advantage of working with someone who's going to help you design the plan is that you probably can get it done more quickly than if you tried to do it yourself.

Start with the vision

The first step is starting with the vision statement. This often trips people up because it involves deep thought about how you want to guide your company into the future. So let's take time and examine this further.

Keep in mind that your vision statement should be broad and grand. It's aspirational and written in the present tense. It should include elements of the following:

- Company core values
- Company culture
- Priorities
- A picture of the future
- Inspiration for your employees
- Passion, as opposed to purpose

Company leaders should embody the vision of the company. It's a critical branding strategy, and your vision should be reflected in all aspects of your company and embraced by everyone who works with you. That last point is essential. Simon Sinek states it best:

"Customers will never love a company until the employees love it first."

Here are some great examples of great vision statements:

- **Feeding America:** "A hunger-free America."
- **IKEA:** "Our vision is to create a better every-day life for many people."
- **Nike:** "Bring inspiration and innovation to every athlete* in the world. (*If you have a body, you are an athlete.)"
- **World Wildlife Fund:** "We seek to save a planet, a world of life. Reconciling the needs of human beings and the needs of others that share the Earth..."
- **Goodwill:** "Every person has the opportunity to achieve his/her fullest potential and participate in and contribute to all aspects of life."
- **UPS:** "Our goal is to synchronize the world of commerce by developing business solutions that create value and competitive advantages for our customers."

Inspired? Make this a team effort. Set aside some time with your employees to dream big. Including them will foster buy-in, and as we all know, employee buy-in is key to success.

One of the most successful business owners I know sets aside the first two weeks in December of every year for strategic planning. She reviews the goals established at the beginning of the year and the adjustments or pivots made along the way. She invites her staff to a three-day retreat away from the office. She hires a facilitator, and each aspect of the business is reviewed, celebrated and adjusted for growth over the next year.

You don't have to hire a facilitator to take your team through the strategic planning process. The key is to be intentional about the activity. Set time apart to review progress, to acknowledge accomplishments, to look forward and to establish clear and measurable goals for the next year.

● TIP #23

USE ACTION PLANS FOR SUCCESS

When I start working with a business client, one of the first questions I ask is, "Do you have an action plan?" Not a strategic plan, although that's very important, too, but an action plan. When they ask me why they need one, I quote Alan Lakein:

"Planning is bringing the future into the present so that you can do something about it now."

> *Have a bias toward action — let's see something happen now. You can break that big plan into small steps and take the first step right away.*
>
> — Indira Gandhi

Here's why I like action plans (and why I think you should too):

1. What gets planned gets done.
2. Plans hold you accountable.
3. Plans keep you focused.

There are many models out there and some pretty good templates, too, but I like a simple one-page action plan. The key is to decide a time frame and make sure your plan has measurable outcomes. The concept of SMART goals is works well for this kind of planning. SMART stands for specific, measurable, achievable, relevant and time-based.

How to write an action plan

In addition to including the obvious who, what, where, when and how in your action plan, I invite you to consider using the elements of my motto when putting your plan together: "Connection, Creativity and Courage."

1. **Connection.** Make sure your plan is relevant to your mission, your goals, and your target audience.
2. **Creativity.** What will you do? How will you do it? How will you be different from your competition?
3. **Courage.** Ask the hard questions. Is this feasible? Is this the right path to take? How will I hold myself and my team accountable?

When you write an action plan

You'll want to formulate an action plan at the beginning of each project. If you have a strategic plan for your business, each section in your plan should have an action plan for implementation. It's important to remember that action plans are not meant to be static. I suggest that you break down the action plan into weekly chunks. The more detailed your plan, the better and the more easily it can be monitored and measured.

How you incorporate an action plan

I've worked with some businesses that use action plans as a reference point in every staff meeting. Each team member reports out what he or she did that week. The beauty of weekly action plans is that they make it easy to course-correct. As you are carrying out the different elements of the action plan and regularly measuring against targets, you can quickly see what is working and what is not.

● TIP #24

PROTECT YOUR INTELLECTUAL PROPERTY

Many small business owners don't do enough to protect their intellectual property. If you have created a system, a design or a process, you should seriously consider legally protecting it. IP (aka intellectual property law) has four primary categories, which are:

> "
> *You know what lasts longer than beauty? Being smart.*
> — Gabrielle Union
> "

1. **Patents.** What you think of when you think of an invention.
2. **Trademarks.** Brand names, or service mark in commerce.
3. **Copyrights.** Original works of authorship like a book, play, film, sculpture or piece of software.
4. **Trade secrets.** Something that is kept confidential by a company for its competitive advantage, such as a customer list or a "secret sauce."

Protecting an idea or product

First, you could file a utility patent. These relate to inventive ideas and are what you usually think of when you hear the word "patent." You get a utility patent on something new, useful or non-obvious — for example, a pharmaceutical compound, a machine or a device.

The second type of intellectual property protection for a product is a design patent. This protects the ornamental design of the product or the industrial design, not the usefulness and utility of a device. For example, you couldn't get a utility patent on the useful aspect of headphones since the technology has been around for a long time, but you could protect the aesthetic design and gain an advantage in the field.

The last type of IP that can be used to protect a product is copyright. It can protect software, mobile apps, movies, books, and other things that are works of authorship. A copyright can be safeguarded and either sold as copies or licensed.

Protecting a brand or logo

You safeguard your brand or logo by filing a trademark. This is is very important to do because your logo controls how people recognize your brand. There are state and federal trademarks. Florida calls it a "fictitious name" and other states call it "DBA" (doing business as).

If you're doing business across state lines, you'll want to file a federal trademark. There are different types of trademarks — one is called a "wordmark," which protects your name, and the other is called a "stylized mark," which protects your logo. Filing for trademark protection will protect you from others using marks that are likely to confuse consumers. It will avoid confusion as to who originated the goods.

When to renew

The copyright only needs to be filed once. However, trademarks must be renewed every 10 years, when you file a statement that you're still using it. As long as the trademark system still exists and you meet the deadline every 10 years, you can do this in perpetuity.

How IP protection can add value

Still questioning whether you need to invest in IP protection? Consider that intellectual property is a tangible asset, just like a piece of property or a building a business would buy. So when you invest in developing IP, it can create value in protecting your product, safeguard your service line and give you opportunities to defend your interest in your market. If you have a competitive advantage in one field, you can protect that and prevent your competitors from conducting activities in that area by filing for an exclusionary right, which helps you exclude others.

Adding value this way benefits you as the market expands or the demand for your product increases, because that tangible asset continues to grow. That asset can then be bought, sold and licensed —and in some circumstances, you can even take a loan against it. This is a great business strategy.

Working with IP attorneys

- Make sure they are looking at your whole business model and understand how you make a profit, how you earn revenue, and how to grow and increase that revenue.
- Choose someone who is going to be your strategic partner as opposed to someone who is just generating expenses.
- If they are looking at a patent, ask how they are going to investigate competitors. Are they going to do prior art searches and search other patents and publications?
- Ask them how they are going to work with you from a business development angle to grow your IP portfolio so it creates value. Equally, if you are working with attorneys on a trademark angle, be sure they are doing proper trademark searches in this country or internationally, depending on your business, so they protect the IP in a way that you can grow your brand and create value while minimizing potential risks.

One of my clients was able to head off a competitor who was a former employee of hers during the bidding process for a contract because she had taken the time to properly protect her IP. She was able to provide background and documents to the contract holder that the process her competitor was proposing actually belonged to her.

CREATE A POLICIES AND PROCEDURES MANUAL

I am often surprised that small business owners don't take the time to create policy manuals and employee handbooks. You know the adage "An ounce of prevention is worth a pound of cure." When you don't take the time to define and disseminate policies and procedures, you can experience real problems.

> *I never dreamed about success. I worked for it.*
>
> — Estée Lauder

Why you need policies and procedures manuals

- They provide direction and guidance.
- They ensure uniformity, which promotes understanding and higher rates of compliance.
- Policies provide internal controls.
- You can use them for training — the more detailed, the better.
- They offer some measure of legal protection by defining the rights and obligations of the employer and the employee. Notice, I said "some measure." Check with your attorneys for policies that have formal regulations.

What these manuals should include

- **The purpose:** Be specific on how policies fit into your overall mission and business development goals
- **The goals and objective:** These can be broad and, if so, should include regularly scheduled evaluation dates.
- **The expectations:** Are these in line with your company's core values?
- **Definitions, if needed:** Each company and each industry has its own language. Put yourself in the place of a brand-new employee. What would that person need to understand?
- **A place to acknowledge receipt of the information:** A signature line for acknowledgment of receipt and review of the document is very important because it protects you from accusations that people did not know what was expected of them.

Criteria for review of the manual

- Be sure to include SMART goals in the policies and procedures. Remember, SMART stands for specific, measurable, attainable, relevant and time-based. It is vital that policies and procedures be implementable. Research, adopt and adapt to policies that meet your company's needs. The good news is that the internet is full of manuals and manual templates that you can adapt to fit your company.

How often you should review your policies and procedures

- It's a good idea to review your policies and procedures at least annually and especially after significant projects or changes in operating systems. Make sure to communicate any updates or changes with employees.

Types of policies and procedures to include

- The sky's the limit, and I say the more, the better. Everyone should be on the same page and know what to expect, especially if employees work at different locations and on multiple projects. Each manual must clearly state the purpose, vision and expectations related to each policy.

Examples of policies and procedures to consider include:

- **Human resources** — Basic information on what each employee is supposed to know about how the company handles jobs and who to go to with any kind of a grievance.
- **Accounting** — Information such as how and when employees get paid.
- **Bonus policies** — Who qualifies for bonuses, along with how and when.
- **Client relations** — Information employees need to know about how clients are acquired, onboarded and exited at the end of a project.
- **Social media** — who is the company's social media administrator? Who monitors the posts and who deals with posts that need to be removed?
- **IT policies** — Who do you contact if there is an IT problem? This policy can outline the procedure for reporting the issue and stop-gap measures so employees can continue to work with minimal interruption.
- **Cybersecurity** — Everyone should know how to spot spam emails that can lead to viruses. Some companies have policies that do not allow the use of USBs because of the potential of viruses. Your policy should also address the rules about ransomware and cyber theft.
- **Vendor selection and payment procedures** — Do you have a supplier diversity policy?
- **Community outreach** — Your employees have favorite organizations they support. Consider having a community outreach policy. This is great for employee engagement and morale. Allowing for time off to volunteer in the community will lead to marketing as an added benefit.
- **Corporate travel and reimbursement** — An outline of what to submit for reimbursement, the required timeframe for requesting payments and how reimbursements are processed. Be sure to include your policy on travel bonus programs. Does the company own hotel points and frequent flier miles, or does the employee get to keep those?
- **Employee evaluations** — An outline of when and how these are

handled and who conducts them. What criteria is being evaluated? Remember to include the appeals process.

- **Internal promotions** — Which circumstances can lead to an employee being promoted, and what criteria is taken into consideration?
- **Confidentiality agreements** — Are your employees able to access information about your clients? Processing payments? Everyone with this kind of access should sign confidentiality agreements.
- **Weapons policy** — What are your state laws? Your company policy should be very clear about your expectations.
- **Conflicts of interest** — Clearly outline what to do if your employees are related to vendors and potential customers.
- **Safety policies** — These should be both general and specific to the type of work.
- **Employee exit interviews** — Although this can sometimes be difficult, employee exit interviews are always a good idea. Your policy manual should outline how these are conducted. Are they face to face? By questionnaire?
- **Personal device use** — Do you want to reimburse employees for using their personal devices? Do you want to allow personal calls and texts during work hours? Your policy manual should clearly define the rules and expectations related to use of personal devices including mobile phones, computers, tablets and other equipment that might be needed for the job.
- **Company equipment use** — The policy should be evident that anything written or searched on company equipment is subject to review. Be very clear about the amount of privacy you allow.
- **Dress code** — This might seem simple, but it's very important for new employees. Is your workplace business casual? Do you allow jeans only on Fridays? Are there specific types of safety gear your company requires?
- **Code of conduct** — Spell out how you expect employees to live up to the values of your company. This might include a policy on alcohol use at work or personal social media posts that can affect the company's reputation.

- **Money management and credit card use** — For employees who have access to corporate funds, what are the parameters they need to know about how money is spent, which approvals are needed and when, and how are transactions recorded?
- **Intellectual property** — Address questions such as who owns what is developed for a client or during office hours or using company equipment. Does it belong to the employee, or does it belong to the company?
- **Industry policies specific to your business** — Include anything employees need to know about required certifications for the job, safety training, federal compliance laws and other information that applies to workers in your field. Which employees are required to abide by these, and which ones are exempt?

Where should policies and procedures manuals be kept?

- The most appropriate location to keep policies and procedures manuals is in a shared file online. That way, they can be accessed by everyone. You may also choose to keep hard copies in a central location in the office.

How do you get buy-in from employees for your policies and procedures?

- The best way to get buy-in is to have your employees included in the drafting, or review or updating of policy manuals. Ask employees to acknowledge receipt, review, and understanding of the policies. They should sign and date the policies. Consider informing your employees that you have an open-door policy for suggested changes. This flexibility will empower them to keep the policies and procedures relevant and implementable.

The good news about policies and procedures manuals is that there are many resources, free samples, and outlines at your disposal. Your industry groups will also have examples you can use. You don't have to hire someone to come in and create the policies if you can't afford to or don't want to do that now. That said, I caution you to reconsider that when you are growing. A solopreneur can operate one way, but a company that has a handful of employees must work very differently.

The bigger your business, the more formal your policies and procedures should become. As mentioned above, I am a big fan of policies and procedures. I believe that what gets written gets done. What gets agreed to gets done. When people understand and embrace expectations, they meet them.

One final thought: Inspect what you expect. Just writing these policies and procedures down and putting the manuals up on a shelf isn't going to cut it. Use these as living documents and you'll see your business blossom and grow as you and your team continue to improve how and why you do things.

FINAL
THOUGHTS

❍ FINAL THOUGHTS

One of my favorite movies is *Hidden Figures*, which is about women of color who were instrumental in the early days of the U.S. space program. What impressed me most about them was their tenacity, determination and confidence that they had the right to be exactly where they were. They knew they had an important role to play, and that inspires me every time I think about their stories.

> *And the day came when the risk to remain tight in a bud was more painful than the risk it took to blossom.*
>
> — Anaïs Nin

I recently saw a picture of five U.S. astronauts who were all women of color. Their accomplishments are partially the result of the women who came before them — the women portrayed in *Hidden Figures* who were known as "human computers." Today's leaders benefit from the education those other women fought to get. Together, all of these women of the space program represent the past, the present and, more importantly, the future. Because of them, young girls will not have to break as many barriers.

Today I invite you to look at your business through the lens of past, present, and future. What obstacles did you overcome? What barriers are you still breaking? Celebrate the fact that you are a woman business owner by getting certified by the Women's Business Enterprise National Council (WBENC), if you haven't already. Once you're certified, you can use the Woman-Owned Logo for further celebration and recognition.

As you consider scaling your business, take stock of who has influenced you. I'll bet if you think about it, you can come up with at least 50 names. Not sure about that?

Start by considering people you know in broad categories:

- Family
- Friends
- Teachers
- Bosses
- Colleagues
- Authors
- Speakers
- Experts and thought leaders

What was it that they did or said or encouraged that influenced you to make the decision to start your business? Do those same sentiments exist as you examine your decision to scale your business?

I hope this book has been useful to you. I hope it has given you ideas and inspiration and, most of all, the knowledge that you are not alone. There are many resources available to help you scale your business. You can decide to scale incrementally, or you may decide to take a really big leap. Whatever your decision, putting some key things in place will not only make the decision easier, it will make the process easier, too.

I also hope you will stay in touch! I've dedicated many years to working with women business owners all over the world. I have a vast network of interesting, experienced and successful women business owners, and I regularly connect with them through coaching, consulting and speaking engagements. They inspire me every day. Their stories have become the fabric of my presentations and workshops and the basis of what I share in my coaching and consulting opportunities. I'd love to add your story to the mix.

Connect with me at nancy@womensbusiness.info.

Thank you for allowing me to share my thoughts with you.

ABOUT THE AUTHOR

Nancy G. Allen is an international speaker, coach, consultant and expert on women's business issues. For more than 30 years, she has been helping small business owners at all stages of growth. As president and CEO of the Women's Business Enterprise Council of Florida, a regional partner of the Women's Business Enterprise National Council, Nancy manages a team of staff, sponsors, partners and women business leaders who are dedicated to certifying, connecting and championing women in business.

Nancy has been recognized for her work on behalf of women in business through numerous prestigious awards, including being named as one of South Florida's 100 most accomplished Caribbean Americans by the International Career and Business Alliance (ICABA); a World Women Leadership Achievement Award from the World Women Leadership Congress; an Association Marketing Award from Women in Ecommerce; and an Honorary Ambassador of Cascais, Portugal, by the Ambassador's Club of the Industry Sector of Cascais and the Estoril Coast.

Her clients have included UPS, the Urban League, AARP, New York Life, State Farm, the Women of Color Empowerment Institute and WEConnect International. Her speaking, training and consulting topics include supplier diversity, negotiation, leadership, strategic planning, strategic alliances and elegant transitions.

Nancy's personal motto is "Connections, creativity and courage in all endeavors." She holds a master's degree from the Johns Hopkins School of Advanced International Studies. Nancy was born in Haiti and raised in South Florida, where she still lives today. She is bilingual in English and French and is fluent in Spanish and Creole.

Made in the USA
Columbia, SC
22 October 2021